Beckley Reflects

The Village greets the Millennium by remembering its past

Compiled by
Peter M. Wheeler

All proceeds from the sale of this book are to benefit local causes

Produced under the auspices of
Beckley and Stowood Parish Council

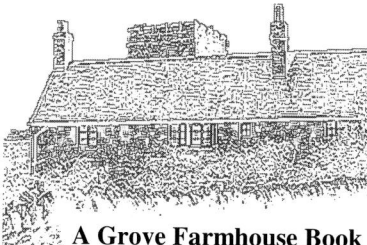

A Grove Farmhouse Book

Published by Bill Broomfield
Grove Farmhouse, Beckley, Oxfordshire, OX3 9US

A catalogue record for this book is available from the British Library.

ISBN 0 9537197 0 7

Printed and bound by Parchment Oxford Ltd,
1a, Crescent Road, Cowley, Oxford.

Contents

A Poem
Foreword by Niall Ferguson
Introduction

Acknowledgements

Picture on front cover: Beckley High Street west end
looking up Chapman's Hill.

I went to Noke
But nobody spoke
I went to Beckley
They spoke directly
At Boarstall and Brill
They all stood still.

I went to Noke
But nobody spoke
I went to Brill
They were silent and still
But I went to Beckley
They spoke directly

I went to Noke
And nobody spoke
I went to Brill
There was silence still
I went to Thame
It was just the same

But I went to Beckley
and they spoke directly.

17th Century verse written by an unknown local writer.

Foreword by Niall Ferguson

**Fellow and Tutor in Modern History,
Jesus College, Oxford.
Author of
The Pity of War
The House of Rothschild
Paper and Iron
*Virtual History***

When Evelyn Waugh heard that he had got a
Third in his Oxford finals, he elected to drown his sorrows in Beckley. He chose well. As I came to appreciate
as an undergraduate, the village on the hill is somehow
out of range of the slings and arrows of the outrageous
university down below.

In the same way, it comes as a delightful relief
for the academic historian to turn from his dry-as-dust
tomes to a book like this. Peter Wheeler and all who
have contributed to *Beckley Reflects* prove, if proof were
needed, that local history - amateur history in the original and best sense - is the vital root of all history.

Beckley is the village it is, unspoilt without being chocolate box, partly because of good luck but mainly because its inhabitants have known how to defend their inheritance. The old rhyme - 'I went to Beckley and they spoke directly' - recalls, among other trials, the hard fight to save Otmoor from the M40.

I hope that all of us who live in or around the village will not only take pleasure from this book, but also draw inspiration. Beckley has been around since the tenth century, when it was 'Becca's Wood'. The approach of the year 2000 is a good time to resolve that it weathers the next ten centuries just as well.

5th September 1999

Introduction

It is not the intention of this book to be a definite history or guide book of the village of Beckley, both of these functions having already been well chronicled in other publications. Although it has been necessary to include some historical details and facts, they have been well supplemented by articles, reminiscences, reflections and memories, call them what you will, of present and past parishioners, and of happenings that have occurred in the Parish, brought together in an effort to show the many varied and some times radical changes that have taken place over the years, mainly within living memory. As years go by memories tend to become hazy and sometimes coloured by imagination, I hope therefore that readers will accept the stories as they are finding some of them amusing whereas some will obviously be sad when people or happenings that are mentioned are gone for ever. It is probably true that many of the stories have the substance of legend, but never the less they are all part of the rich pattern that goes to make up the social history of our village.

The book owes many of its roots to the excellent booklet published in 1965 by the Beckley Women's Institute entitled "Signpost to Beckley, A portrait of the village in 1965," which was based on an award winning scrapbook. Also an idea of a past editor of the Beckley Parish Newsletter Nigel Purse, who in January 1996 suggested that interesting articles from the Newsletter be brought together in book form. It seemed appropriate therefore, as we approached the end of the millennium that it was an opportune time to write about the notable events and our memories, and collecting them all together before they are forgotten.

I am indebted to, and wish to thank all those who have helped me with the preparation of this book by providing articles, photographs, information and advice, without them it would not have been possible and I hope I have remembered to give everyone their due credit, but please accept my sincere apologies if you have been inadvertently overlooked. Both Phyllis and I have enjoyed recalling and recording our memories, and encouraging others to do likewise. Personally I feel very privileged to be allowed to put it all together, a task that has given me great deal of pleasure.

Peter M.Wheeler.

Chapter One

Beckley, Literally

A Village of inspiration

Beckley has several notable literary connections whose individual efforts have been inspired and enhanced by working in and around the village.

Cripps Cottage in Otmoor Lane was immortalised by **R.D.Blackmore (1825-1900)** in his novel *Cripps the Carrier*. The book written in 1877 recalls the times when the carrier was the link between the village and the town, these men were of the utmost importance to the residents as they would deliver and/or collect almost anything (including passengers) in the course of their journeys. In 1904 there were four in the village working back and forth to Oxford on various days. The last one, a Mr. Willis, who lived in Common Road (in the house now called Whistlers) operated until the late 1930's.

John Buchan (1875-1940) the first Baron Tweedsmuir bought Elsfield Manor, several properties and land in and around Beckley including Noke Wood in 1919. Several residents of the parish worked for him as gamekeepers, grooms and domestic servants. He lived at Elsfield until his appointment as Governor-General of Canada in *1935*. His novel *Midwinter* is set in the area around our village. Although he was a prolific writer he is probably best remembered for his novels *The Thirty Nine Steps* and *Greenmantle* that were both made into successful films. The title of *The Thirty Nine Steps* was suggested by the number of steps on the staircase at Elsfield Manor.

The view from Beckley across the chequered fields of Otmoor supposedly inspired **Charles Dodgson (1832-1898)** better known by his pseudonym **Lewis Carroll**, to include the giant chessboard in his book *Alice through* the *Looking Glass*. The particular panorama viewed by Dodgson no doubt from the 'Duffus' field, is now sadly no more, most of the hedgerows having been removed in the interests of modern farming.

This photograph was taken looking up Church Street outside the old post office, now New Ridge. Lindum Cottage with its thatch looking rather worse for wear is on the right. The church tower is just visible as is also the thatched roof of the barn that was where the pedestrian school entrance is now. The man standing by the gate to the barn is Mr Gatz who was the village baker. The barn collapsed during a violent storm in the early 1930's. Some of the people in the photograph were identified by Annie Wing, who died in 1978. She is in the back row extreme right, her appearance looks as though she was probably in her early teens and as she was born in 1887 would date the photograph in the early 1900's.

Evelyn Waugh (1903-1966)

Author of many works including *Brideshead Revisited*, used the Abingdon Arms as a retreat where he could write in an atmosphere of peace and quiet whilst enjoying the landlady's (Mrs Lizzie Mattingley) legendary hospitality.

Extracts from the diaries of Evelyn Waugh. (1903 - 1966)
Evelyn Waugh came down from Oxford in the summer of 1924. When he re-visited the area he regularly stayed at the Abingdon Arms, sometimes in a caravan in the garden.

Written on 1st September 1924.
On Sunday 27th July I left London quite suddenly for Beckley. I arrived at Beckley in the late evening having walked all the way from the station bearing a bag and found Alastair in the caravan. We spent a quiet evening in the pub.
I got back to the caravan (29th July) to find Alastair already arrived....we went to dinner with Squire Cooke *(my great uncle who lived* at *the Grove at this time)* who had a nephew Tommy Beechcrofts elder brother - staying with him. He gave us some admirable ducks grown by Mr. Higgs *(Local farmer - editors note)* and plenty to drink. When he had lapsed into muttering we went home to the caravan.

Wednesday 28th July 1924.
There was a big feast on at Beckley to which we had been invited. First there were sports and a cricket match and then at four an enormous meal in the big barn next to the pub. From then until about three in the morning the whole village sat and ate and drank and danced and sang. It was a most delightful

evening. Harold Claire *(Local farmers son - editors note)* was very, very drunk, but an excellent host to Alastair and myself, continually filling our glasses and introducing us to people. We danced with Mrs. Mattingley   several times and drank pints of beer. Mr. Higgs was well drunk. Cooke came in for a little and embraced a small boy.

A party of villagers outside the Oddfellows Barn. The occasion was to celebrate the Diamond Jubilee of Queen Victoria in 1897. The Reverend Doyne is in the centre wearing a mortar board. The Oddfellows barn was opposite the Abingdon Arms and next to Shipley Cottage, it was used for village activities until after the Second   World war when it was pulled down to make room for Abingdon Cottages.

Thursday 29th July - Saturday 30th August 1924.
In the morning I had my viva.... I telegraphed to my parents to

inform them of my certain third and returned much dispirited to Beckley. *(Next morning)...* rode back to Beckley where we drank champagne.... It was a very drunken night at the Abingdon Arms. Next day we dined with Cooke and Harold, and he and Mrs. Mattingley came back to the caravan when the pub shut and drank champagne with us and Alastair and I gave a brooch to Mrs. Mattingley which we had bought at Paynes.

Mrs Lizzie Mattingley with her son Reg
landlady of the Abingdon Arms between the wars.

We went to Beckley for half an hour to call for a stick Alastair had left there. Mrs. Mattingley gave us a drink and told us the village gossip. It seems that Cooke is really selling his house. Mr. Higgs, who had never left Oxfordshire, went to the Empire Exhibition at Wembley and returned very drunk but much impressed with it's beauty and grandeur. We called on Cooke and drank with him.

Saturday 29th August 1925.

I left Barford in Alastair's car, meaning to go to London from Oxford. We lunched in Banbury on bread and cheese and then went to Beckley where everyone was so sweet that I decided to spend the night there. Cooke has been away and looks a little better than when I last saw him. Harold Claire has nearly killed himself in his car again.

Abingdon Arms c.1905

Beckley Sunday 30th August 1925.

It was pleasant waking up in Beckley. I sat in the inn porch reading a newspaper until 12 when Mr. Cooke and Mr. Higgs came down for their morning drink. At lunchtime Alastair arrived from Barford and we ate roast pork and celery with Mr. Cooke. Cooke without saying a word to me, paid for my board and lodging. I thought it was extraordinarily sweet of him...

The Abingdon Arms, Beckley, Oxon. Tuesday 23rd August 1927.
I came here rather suddenly ten days ago... .1 go into Oxford most days to work in the Union Library....Beckley is very much altered. Old Cooke is dead. I have been surprised to realize how little I want to go and sit in the parlour in the evenings now he isn't there. Harold Claire has left the village and is reported badly of by everyone. Only Mr. Higgs survives. He got very drunk the other evening and giggled and tried to dance with Mrs. Mattingley....

The Diaries of Evelyn Waugh. Edited by Michael Davie.
Published by Wiedenfeld and Medson. Orion Publishing Group Ltd.

The Abingdon Arms

Chapter Two

A Brief History

There are in the Ashmolean Museum in Oxford several objects found in our village, dating back to the Bronze Age and some from the Iron Age. This seems to indicate that there were people choosing to live here in prehistoric times.

There is no firm record of either the Ancient Britons or the early Romans ever having a settlement here, but it seems inconceivable, that such a prime hilltop site, with fine views all around to make it easily defended, would not have been used.

The Romans built a road through the area, which thankfully, is the only road that has ever crossed Otmoor. The road ran from Dorchester in the south to Alcester, a Roman town 2 miles south of Bicester, in the north, and was part of the extensive network of roads built by the Romans. It was an essential route linking Towcester on Watling Street, with Silchester, between Reading and Basingstoke. If you walk along the line of the road on Otmoor it is not difficult to imagine a Roman Legion marching across, the Centurion shouting orders, and the men no doubt grumbling as soldiers do. Perhaps they were on their way to one of the northern garrisons and looking forward to a break and a meal at Alcester. The legionnaires were very fit and well able to march up to 30 miles in a day, but it must have been very hard for men from a Mediterranean climate to adapt to our cold and damp British weather. The fact that the Romans built a road across the moor tends to endorse the theory that it was not always so prone to flooding, they were apparently averse to getting their sandals wet! Near the centre of the moor is what little remains of Joseph's Stone, it is (among other things) thought to be a Roman milestone. (see further comment in the section on Otmoor.)

During the Roman occupation a villa was built near the footpath leading to Upper, Middle and Lower Park Farms (Beckley Park), sadly, no remains are left today. All traces were destroyed soon after it was discovered in 1862. Despoilers and vandals have wrought their havoc through every age and generation whether motivated by politics, religion or economics, or perhaps by the sheer need to destroy something. Apparently it was not such a grand villa as some built in other parts of the County, but one wonders what possessed the perpetrators to completely obliterate the site. When the native population had been subdued, (apart from those on the other side of Hadrian's Wall and in the far west of course,) many Romans came to settle in Britain, I imagine that the occupier of the villa was one of these, possibly someone involved in local administration, or perhaps the owner of the iron smelting works that was near Woodeaton, or even a wealthier native Briton following the Roman traditions. Smaller roads linked the villa and Woodeaton to the main road. The site of the villa enjoys some of the best views for many miles around, and it would have been splendid if at least some of the remains could have been preserved.

The power of the Roman Empire gradually declined, and due to unrest at home, early in the 4th century AD the military legions were withdrawn leaving Britain to the mercy of the native Celts, the Saxons, Vikings and other invaders. Many of the settlers returned home rather than face the coming lawlessness without the protection of the Roman

Legions. This situation of colonial settlers having to leave, even after several generations, and descendants having never seen the land of their forebears has been repeated through history, right up to modern times. The ones with the most to fear were the Britons who had prospered under Roman rule,

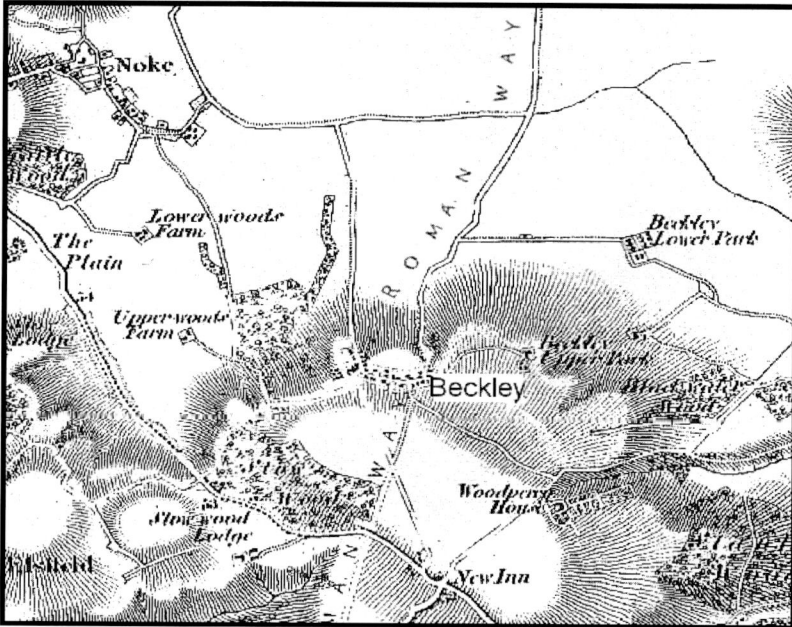

Reproduced from 1st edition 1833, Banbury and Buckingham 1 inch to 1 mile map by permission of Ordnance Survey on behalf of the Controller of Her Majesty's Stationary Office, © Crown Copyright Licence No. MC99/175

they had nowhere to go and faced a very uncertain future.

During the next five centuries anarchy reigned in the country when invading armies from all over Europe fought each other for ascendancy. In consequence what happened in Beckley at this time is somewhat obscure. It was not until Alfred the Great's victories in the 9th century that comparative peace was restored. We then find a mention in the 10th century of a settlement in a clearing in the thick forest that covered the area, it was called Becca's Wood. Who then, was

Becca? We can only guess. I have always imagined him to be a Saxon who perhaps had served in Alfred's army fighting against the Vikings, and he may have been given the land as a reward for loyal service. The parish was one of several in the area believed at one time to be owned by King Alfred but this was later proved to be untrue.

Life in the settlement could not have been easy, Viking raids were still an occasional danger, and the quest for food and fuel was always of prime importance. The inhabitants had no shops when they wanted supplies. Although the woods were full of deer and wild boar Otmoor had lots of wildfowl and the River Ray plenty of fish and eels, they all had to be caught. Wood fuel for cooking and warmth was plentiful in the forest, but had to be felled and drawn home. In later years the produce of the forest, moor and rivers became the property of the Crown or local Overlords. Life for the ordinary people became even harder, with dire consequences meted out to those caught poaching. It is difficult to imagine just how they survived.

Although Christianity was established in Britain during Roman times, and surprisingly tolerated by their administration, it wasn't until the 6th or 7th century that it became universally accepted. Sometime after this our first church in Beckley was built of wood on the same site as the present building.

Beckley has a Holy Well the waters of which were once reputed to have healing properties. It is called Saint Tinniver's Well and is situated in the bank to the north of the High Street. Little is known about the Saint the well is named after, other than that he was an early English martyr who died in the post-Roman time (after 440 AD) and was buried in Beckley. His shrine, which was most likely on the site of the present church, was visited by pilgrims and revered for many centuries. He was also known by a Celtic name of St Donanverdh. Our local Councils have commemorated the Saint by naming two houses built not far from the well ' St Tinniver's Cottages.'

In the 11th century came the Norman Conquest and Beckley became the capital of Otmoor being certainly the largest of the 'seven towns.' The others were Noke, Oddington, Charlton on Otmoor, Fencott, Murcott and Horton cum Studley. A Norman, Roger d'Ivry together with his 'sworn brother' Robert d'Oily who married the daughter of a local Saxon lord, became the overlords of Beckley. It is possible that the name d'Oily became changed over the years to Deely, a family who owned property in the area, and a name quite common in the Otmoor region.

High Street Beckley

13

The Domesday Book

Beckley was recorded in the Doomsday Survey of 1085 which set out the details of population and cultivated lands. In 1066 when William of Normandy invaded and conquered England, he was crowned King and the lands of the English nobles were granted to his followers. In 1085 William decided to carry out a survey in each Shire, to find out what - or how much each landholder held - in land and livestock, and what it was worth. The commissioners responsible for the survey, were given the following brief :-

THE NAME OF THE PLACE. WHO HELD IT BEFORE 1066 AND NOW? HOW MANY HIDES, HOW MANY PLOUGHS, BOTH THOSE IN LORDSHIP AND THE MEN'S? HOW MANY VILLAGERS, COTTAGERS AND SLAVES? HOW MUCH WOODLAND, MEADOW AND PASTURE? HOW MANY MILLS AND FISHPONDS? HOW MUCH HAS BEEN ADDED OR TAKEN AWAY? WHAT THE TOTAL VALUE WAS AND IS? HOW MUCH EACH FREE MAN HAD OR HAS? WHAT THE TOTAL VALUE WAS AND IS? ALL THREEFOLD BEFORE 1066, WHEN KING WILLIAM GAVE IT, AND NOW; AND IF MORE CAN BE HAD THAN AT PRESENT? THE RETURNS WERE TAKEN TO WILLIAM AT WINCHESTER, BEFORE HE LEFT ENGLAND FOR THE LAST TIME IN 1086.

The entry for our village was as follows:-

Bechelie, Oxenefscire.

Rogerivs de jvri,ten Bechelie. Ibi st. VI. HID'. Tra. VII.car. Ncin dnio II.car. 7XI. uitti cu. VI.bord hnt. v car. Ibi xx. ac pti. 7 paftura. 1. lueIg. 7 II.qrent lat. Silua.

TRANSLATION :
BECKLEY OXFORDSHIRE

ROGER OF IVRY HOLDS BECKLEY. 6 HIDES. LAND FOR 7
PLOUGHS. NOW IN LORDSHIP 2 PLOUGHS; 6 SLAVES. 11
VILLAGERS WITH 6 SMALLHOLDERS HAVE 5 PLOUGHS.
MEADOW, 20 ACRES; PASTURE 1 LEAGUE LONG AND 2
FURLONGS WIDE; WOODLAND 1 LEAGUE LONG AND 1/2 A
FURLONG WIDE. THE VALUE WAS 100S; NOW £8.

Notes on the entry:-
HIDÆ. (hide) The English unit of land measurement or assessment, often
reckoned as 120 acres.
CARUCA. (car) A plough together with the oxen who pull it, usually 8.
LEUGA. (league) A measure of length, usually about a mile and a half.
VILLA. (village or town) Translated from the old English Tun or town.
There was not at that time any distinction between small villages or large
towns.
***Reproduced by kind permission from the Phillimore Edition of
Domesday Book (General Editor John Morris) volume 14 Oxfordshire,
published in 1978 by Phillimore and Co Ltd, Shopwyke Manor Barn,
Chichester, West Sussex PO20 6BG.***

The Lord of the Manor Roger of Ivry, was the 'sworn
brother' of Robert d'Oilly with whom he jointly held much
land, probably including areas around Beckley. Rogers wife
was Azelina, daughter of Hugh of Grandmesnil. Robert
d'Oilly was Sheriff of Warwickshire, Oxfordshire and it is
thought Berkshire. He was the builder and keeper of Oxford
Castle.
The Palace was built during this time, in the field behind
the present Old Manor Farmhouse, a site which has
magnificent views. It is not certain exactly when it was built,
but in view of the association with the village of the D'Ivry's
and D'Oilly's it seems certain that these rich Norman families

were associated with the building during a period of over a hundred years. It is also likely that the St Valery family was involved at some time. This was a period of intrigue and instability with all the Lords and Barons bickering and fighting among themselves. The various trials and tribulations of Beckley in those years and Royal involvement in following years are ably set out in the booklet by Mr P.D.Cresswell, 'An English Village, Beckley near Oxford'. The Palace for some unknown reason, fell into disrepair in the 16th century and was never rebuilt. According to writers in the early 19th century, the moat and earthworks were visible at that time and there was still standing a stone tower used as a dovehouse. In the Middle Ages doves were raised extensively for food, much to the chagrin of the peasant farmers whose crops suffered the depredations of the birds. An interesting point is that the field where the palace once stood is known as the Duffers or Duffus (dovehouse) field. It is certain that many of the older Beckley cottages and walls contain stone once used in the Palace buildings. If only those stones could talk, what tales they would no doubt tell!

There is a story, that on the death of Henry the First in 1135, Stephen de Blois and Henrys daughter Matilda both contested the throne. A virtual state of civil war existed between them, during which Stephen besieged Matilda in Oxford Castle. She escaped however, during extreme winter weather, by walking across the frozen moat and the River Thames to Wallingford. On the way Matilda was reputed to have stopped at Beckley for rest and refreshment, this stay would have probably been at the palace as the hunting lodge at Beckley Park was not built until later, although the history of the palace and the lodge seem to have often become mixed and confused in the passages of time.

The Normans, as was their custom, rebuilt the church in stone, setting out the layout almost as it is today. The North wall of the present chancel is all that remains of the original Norman church.

Beckley Park was originally built as a hunting lodge probably as early as 1175. Later in the century a circular wall was built around the park, which was then stocked with deer. An examination of the Ordnance Survey map of the district clearly shows the area enclosed by the wall. Subsequent years saw the Park's good hunting enjoyed by the Kings of England especially after the Manor reverted to the ownership of the Crown. The present building was erected in 1540 by Sir John Williams who later became Lord Williams of Thame. His descendants by following a rather unusual line of succession through the Norreys family, were created Earls of Abingdon and retained the property until it was sold in 1920 to the Fielding family. During the late 19th century when the house and its lands were let, farmer Ted Hall's brother walked

Beckley Park

across the fields to be married in Beckley Church, returning to the house in the same way with his bride, after the ceremony.

In the 13th Century there was a windmill known as Lords Mill situated roughly between Foxhill Farm and the present TV mast. The field is shown on old maps as Mill Field. In the 17th Century there was another mill belonging to the vicar, presumably on or near the same site.

There is no firm evidence of Beckley being directly involved in the Civil War other than perhaps the cause of the findings in the churchyard noted elsewhere in this journal. It would be strange however, given the closeness of the Royalist headquarters in Oxford, that our village would not have suffered at some time during the conflict. The fact also was that much skirmishing took place between Wheatley and Islip, on the old main turnpike road from Worcester to London, (now the B4027).

In June 1643 The Earl of Essex made an attack on Islip which was repulsed. A Royalist force under Prince Rupert made up mostly of cavalry, were in the area around Beckley and were very annoyed at having missed this engagement, in reprisal they mounted a raid on Chinnor which then led on to the "Battle of Chalgrove Field" and the subsequent death of John Hampden. On another occasion a Royalist troop from Woodperry drove the sheep from Horton Common presumably to provide food. All of this activity in our area tends to the belief that we could not in any way have escaped involvement. The local farms and homesteads would certainly have been looted by both forces to provide food. In those days armies had no proper supply system, the troops having to forage what they could from the land they passed through, a method that regularly left the local population starving.

Interestingly, the house names on the old turnpike road past Stowood, tell us that they were all coaching inns at some time, White House, New Inn, Royal Oak and the Red Lion, if they were all open at the same time, the competition for custom must have been extremely fierce.

Wick Farm on the edge of Barton Estate is just inside Beckley and Stowood Parish and was a farming community in the 13th Century. Remains of much earlier Roman occupation was found to the north of the farm on the line of the Roman road. Wick Farmhouse was rebuilt after a fire destroyed most of it in 1840 and in the yard is an extraordinary well house built around 1660.

It is widely thought that Grove House was built by Edward Bee who was a wealthy silk merchant. There is a theory however that it was built much earlier by a Spanish family of London Bankers from whom Edward Bee bought The Grove, several cottages in Church Street and about 500 acres of land including Noke Wood. Bee Cottage in Church Street was supposedly used by Edward Bee to house his domestic staff, he also rebuilt the front of The Grove in Georgian style and laid out the gardens. From early 1820 until 1925 the house was occupied by the Cooke family who had

Grove House

inherited it from the Bees and for part of the time it served as the Vicarage. In 1925 it was bought by the Hon. Holland-Hibbert who lived there until his death in 1961. Mrs Holland-Hibbert sold the house in 1976.

In the early 1880's two homes for orphans were opened by Miss Caroline Cooke, whose brother was both squire and vicar living at Grove House. One for boys was called Oldridge near the church, now Grove Farmhouse, the other for girls was called Newridge and was in Church Street. This house, between the wars was the village Post Office and shop, kept by the Wing family.

Wick Farm well head

Jurassic Beckley   By Frank Ratford

About four years ago I was sifting some sand which I had taken from the outside of a fox's lair when I happened to find a sharp flint knife, about 4" long and 1/2" wide. It was shaped like a slim wedge with a very sharp cutting edge. It was taken to Woodstock Museum where it was identified (as I had suspected) as a Stone Age 'flensing' knife, and dated around 1100BC. It would have been used to cut the skin from the flesh of small animals.

Another much older find came from the spoil around a badger's sett. This is a piece of corallian rag or soft coral limestone which has the imprint of a well-defined leaf fossil. Again it was taken to the museum where it was dated as being from the Jurassic period, that is about one hundred and sixty million years ago. As the find was made at the 350ft contour line, this indicates that at that time Beckley was a small coral island or peninsular surrounded by a warm coral sea whose shore was 350 ft higher than our present sea level. Much of the village and surrounding countryside would have been submerged.

There was further evidence to support this view as I found a fine specimen of a "Devils toe-nail" (a large warm water oyster shell) near the same spot. The leaf fossil is remarkably like our beech leaf, which suggests that deciduous trees stood near the shoreline.

To give some idea of the enormous timescales involved, I have calculated the following equivalent comparisons :-

IF ONE MINUTE EQUALS
ONE THOUSAND YEARS
then
TWO MINUTES EQUALS
THE TIME SINCE THE BIRTH OF CHRIST.
THE AGE OF THE FOSSILS
WOULD BE FIFTY FIVE DAYS
and (wait for it !)...
THE SPAN OF A PERSON'S LIFE
WOULD PASS BY IN **FOUR** SECONDS !!

Frank Ratford 1993.

Beckley Time

The Bertie and Grove Estate Sales

Following the Great War of 1914-18, two significant happenings took place which caused big social changes in Beckley. In 1919 Viscount Bertie of Thame offered his extensive family estates in Horton and Beckley for sale, followed in 1921 by the Cooke family doing the same with their properties. The two sales were very wide ranging extending from Beckley Park, the Abingdon Arms, The Grove, many farms and farm land, most of the cottages in the village and Noke Wood.

One can speculate on the reasons for the sales, maybe due to the bad economic situation following the war, or perhaps even the big landowners considering it time to reform the 'tied' system that had existed for many years . One thing however is sure, it was the beginning of a radical change in our social history when individual house ownership became normal practice, and thankfully marked the end of a virtual feudal system.

Chapter Three

The Village at War

The sounds of war came early to Beckley. In the early 1930's a High level bombing range was established on Otmoor, and villagers became used to the sound of aircraft and exploding bombs. The aircraft in those days were small with single engines, biplanes such as the Hawker Hart and Hind and the single wing Fairy Battle and Vickers Wellesley. The aircraft and the practice bombs were not nearly so noisy as those that were to follow later. The range was manned by about a dozen RAF men living in Nissen type huts situated at the bottom of Otmoor Lane near Lower Farm. In addition to the living quarters there was an observation tower, from where hits or misses on a white painted wooden target, situated in the middle of the moor, could be recorded. A similar tower near Horton, manned from Beckley when bombing was taking place, recorded the bomb bursts at 90 degrees from the Beckley tower. Originally the range was administered by 101 (Bomber) Squadron based at Bicester and in 1936 was transferred to Upper Heyford. In 1940 Upper Heyford was formed into No 16 Operational Training Unit Comprising Nos. 7 and 76 Squadrons using the Otmoor range for bombing practice. The following months saw aircraft from many of the wartime airfields that sprang up around Oxfordshire, Buckinghamshire and surrounding Counties using Otmoor on which to practice dropping their bombs.

When war seemed inevitable, a party of evacuees arrived from London, each with their hand luggage, gas masks and name labels pinned to their coats. They gathered at the school to be allocated their foster homes. The local children stared in wonder at these bewildered, homesick youngsters from Holborn, who could well have arrived from another planet. After much deliberation, the newcomers were allocated their new homes. Some of the friendships subsequently formed between villagers and the evacuees still endure today.

On September 3rd 1939, the Prime Minister's 11.00am radio announcement of the declaration of war, was followed

Beckley Civil Defence. Air Raid Wardens, 1940
Back row from left; Eddie Charlett, Peter Blencowe, Henry Wakelin,
Ron Jacobs, Arthur Whiting. Front row from left; Alf Sumner, Alf
Senior, Amos Wing, Hector Wheeler, Harold Lambourne, Jim Anstiss

26

almost immediately by the wailing of the Oxford air raid sirens sounding the 'Alert'. The Beckley Air Raid Wardens toured the village on bicycles and on foot, blowing their whistles and exhorting their neighbours to "Take cover as quickly as you can". Fortunately on this occasion it was a false alarm and the "All Clear" was sounded shortly after.

During the remainder of 1939 and early 1940 there was little to indicate that there was a war on. Some villagers joined the forces and many of the evacuees drifted back to London. The evacuation of our army from France however, and the imminent possibility of a German invasion, made everyone realise that we were now truly at war.

On the 14th of May 1940, the government broadcast an appeal for able bodied men between the ages of 17 and 65 to volunteer to help repulse the expected invasion. The organisation was to be called the Local Defence Volunteers. The appeal was made by the Secretary of State for War, Anthony Eden who went on to say "This name describes its duties in three words. You will not be paid, but you will receive uniforms and will be armed. In order to volunteer, what you have to do is give your name at your local police station, and then, when we want you, we will let you know." The response was instantaneous and astounding, within twenty four hours of the broadcast around a quarter of a million men had registered, and by the end of June the figure was 1,456,000. Inevitably, in the aftermath of the defeat in France, the War Office was desperately trying to reorganise the Regular and Territorial forces and distribute their much reduced resources to meet the expected onslaught. In consequence the LDV had a very low priority, and local units were left pretty much to arm and organise themselves. The only early official concession was the issue of armbands stencilled with the letters LDV. Problems that were most urgent were, the shortage of weapons and uniforms, the lack of competent instructors, and finding suitable times when the majority could attend training sessions. This was at a time when industrial hours were being increased for the war effort, and of course when haymaking and harvesting was at its height. All types of firearms were brought out and in our village there was a fairly good supply of shotguns and sporting rifles.

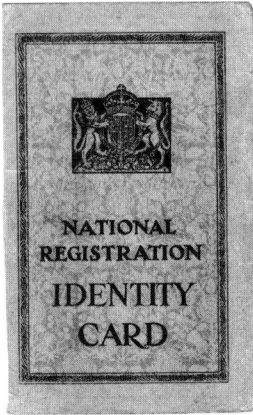

At the insistence of the Prime Minister Winston Churchill, the force was later renamed The Home Guard (Dads Army), and until uniforms and rifles became available, it was decided that the role of the force would be simply to observe anything unusual in their locality, check and question strangers with the object of limiting the activities of spies and "Fifth Columnists", and quickly pass all information to the Police or Military Authorities. As a result of this instruction the force was nicknamed the "Look, Duck and Vanishers". The Fifth Column was a tactic the Germans had used successfully in Poland, Norway, The Low Countries, Belgium and France by infiltrating troops in civilian disguises to disrupt communications, transport and essential supplies in advance of the invading armies. Many stories abounded, one being that parachutists dressed as nuns had been seen descending, as a consequence many real nuns came under suspicion some times with hilarious results, but more often with acute embarrassment. A unit of the Home Guard was formed in Beckley under the command of Captain The Hon Holland Hibbert. Dickie Lethbridge was Sergeant, Hubert Atkins and Arthur Clarke Corporals. The old W.I. room at Grove House, now part of Grove Cottage, was used as the headquarters and guard room of the Beckley unit. A small hut formed an observation post on the footpath to Upper Park Farm, this provided a view for miles over the surrounding countryside and was manned from dusk until dawn. Although I was not old enough at that time to join, I and other village lads were

Beckley Home Guard 1941
From left, Back row ; Joe Tompkins, Tony Walker, Ken Williams, Leslie Little. Middle row Frank Rawlings, not known, Tom Hall, Bert Crawford, not known, Norman Clarke, Bill Payne. Front row; John Wilson, Hubert Atkins, Dickie Lethbridge, The Hon. Holland-Hibbert, Arthur Clarke, Harry Smith, Jock Mackay.

asked to use our bicycles and act as messengers between the two places, a task we thoroughly enjoyed (very few radios and no mobile phones then of course). The lane up to the hut was much rougher then than now, and it was very hazardous for cycling in the 'black out' with no lights! Open fields were dotted with old cars, or planted with large posts to obstruct the expected landings by parachutists and gliders. Sandbagged gun emplacements (although remember the only guns we had were 12 bores and sporting rifles.) were erected at key points, one by the church gate, another behind the wall of what is now the Abingdon Arms car park. Big tree trunks were fitted with cart wheels so they could be swung across to block the roads. Part of the ironwork support of one of these can still be seen, cemented low down in the stone wall between the Grove House gate and Church Corner. I sometimes wonder how long these roadblocks or our little guns would have delayed the German Panzers, but at the time it was good to be doing something that at least seemed positive. The normal ringing of church bells was banned after the German occupation of France so that in the event of an invasion they could be rung as a warning to the population. This occurred in the middle of the night of September 7th 1940, and everyone got up thinking that it was the 'big one'. This however, proved to be a false alarm, although many rumours circulated about landings taking place on the South coast and being repulsed by setting fire to oil on the surface of the sea, so engulfing the invading landing barges. Apparently it was just a rumour but there is no doubt it was an invaluable boost to our morale in those particularly dark and depressing days.

Gradually for the volunteers, supplies improved, the arm bands were augmented by denim overalls and then replaced by khaki battle dress. Shoulder flashes bore the words "Home

Guard" with the units County of origin and Battalion Number. The most important additions were of course the weapons, Lee Enfield and Ross rifles came first followed by Thompson, Sten and Bren machine guns. Gradually more sophisticated weapons became available, especially in the anti-tank and anti-aircraft range, although the latter, not of course necessary in our village. After the cessation of hostilities in Europe, the force was stood down and finally disbanded in the Autumn of 1945.

We did not see much of the Battle of Britain other than occasionally sighting aircraft vapour trails high in the sky accompanied by sounds of distant machine gun fire. The consequences however, could be seen at the side of Garsington Road at Cowley, where an ever growing pile of shot down German planes were stacked. The Metal Produce Recovery Department (MPRD) of the Morris Works processed the scrap to be re-used, ironically, in the making of more aircraft for the RAF to fight the Germans.

The villagers then listened night after night to the distinctive engine beat of German aircraft overhead on their way to bomb cities and towns in the Midlands and North. During the attacks on Coventry and Birmingham the northern sky was lit up by the glow of fires. The heavy raids on London saw the return of the evacuees, many of their parents also moved into the village, the fathers with jobs in London coming down at weekends. A young evacuee, the first black boy that many of us had seen, was billeted with Mrs Jones in Church Street. His name was David Williams but everyone called him Sambo, to which no one thought of objecting, much less Sam himself. He was quite happy and got on well with everyone and we with him without a thought of colour prejudice, he was just 'one of us'. Without a doubt, today we would be in dire trouble with the Race Relations people for calling him what we did.

During this time Otmoor bombing range was fitted with lights to represent the runways of an airfield. The lights were switched on and off during the German raids to coax the Luftwaffe (German Air Force) to waste their bombs on the moor, It was hoped that some of the bombers would pick an 'easy' target and dump their bombs on the moor rather than face

The RAF Tower
at the bottom of Otmoor lane

the anti-aircraft gunfire over the towns and cities. Records show that during The hours of darkness on 2nd September 1940 the Germans dropped five high explosive bombs on Weston-on-the-Green airfield and one on Otmoor Bombing Range, probably the first of many dropped here over the next few years! Many of the ensuing bombs must have been big ones because even whilst exploding in the soft clay, they made a lot of noise. After the war when the moor was swept for unexploded bombs, a lot of German as well as British were unearthed, so the ruse had been successful.

The village had a near miss when two German bombs exploded in a field off Otmoor Lane, due again to the soft clay soil no damage was caused other than making large craters. In fact until the following morning, many villagers were unaware that any bombs had fallen, others heard the whistle as they fell, but had no idea that they had been close enough to deposit lumps of clay in some gardens. Had they burst on the road, 30 yards or so further east, there would not have been a window left intact in Beckley.

On one occasion when the decoy lights were on, a Whitley bomber, returning from a raid over Europe, damaged and with its radio out of action, made a crash landing on the moor mistaking it for a real airfield. It was believed at the time to be a German aircraft and the sound of machine gun fire was heard as it came over. Apparently the RAF men on the tower also thinking it was German, shot at it with their Lewis gun as it came in to land. The Beckley Home Guard were turned out to round up the crew, Rob Jones and 'Boxer' Merchant who lived at the bottom of Church Street were cycling up the street to join the platoon, when Rob stopped to pump up a flat tyre, leaning his bicycle against the well rail. The corporal, Hubert Atkins, who was gardener at Grove House, came running down the street and shouted, "Come on, you haven't time to pump up that tyre, there are b..... Jerries on Otmoor !" It is not on record what expletives he used when the squad, all keyed up to arrest 'the enemy' were met by the aircrew, led by the pilot carrying a small dog under his arm, calling greetings in typical British voices. After a few weeks the bomber was repaired, took off and flew back to its home base.

As the war progressed, larger twin and then four engined aircraft and bigger noisier bombs were used. After 1942 the United States Air Force occasionally used the range, and fortunately, in view of their widely held reputation for inaccuracy, and probably happily for the Otmoor villages, not very often. Considering how close the range was to the village, and that it was in use twenty four hours a day, not many bombs were actually dropped in Beckley. The most serious incident occurred in 1943, when in the early hours of one morning, a large cluster bomb containing many smaller incendiary bombs was dropped on the bottom end of Church Street. The roof of what is now Midsummer Cottage was hit and set on fire, bombs were burning all around, on the road, in gardens, fields, and orchards, but fortunately no more houses were hit, especially when you remember that there were five more cottages at the bottom end of Church Street that had thatched roofs at that time, Henry Wakelin's hayricks down the lane had a near escape when one of the bombs exploded alongside, but the hay was protected by a bent sheet of corrugated iron and the bomb like all the others around burnt out harmlessly. Meanwhile the cottage roof was going well. tackled by neighbours using buckets and the wartime hand stirrup pumps, it was a hopeless task. With no mains water, buckets had to be carried down from the well further up the street, and pumped by hand from wells at nearby cottages. They tried hard to keep the fire from spreading, without success. Arthur Williams, the local baker, had earlier dashed into the cottage to bring out the kitchen table drawer containing the Jones family's precious ration books. A National Fire Service crew finally arrived just as dawn was breaking, and the chief fire officer, who had also been up all night, curtly ordered everyone off the site. This upset one of the exhausted villagers who had been fighting the fire, and he asked the officer why they had taken so long to respond. An altercation ensued which threatened to get out of hand, only quick action and soothing words from other villagers present, prevented the two men from coming to blows. It was said that

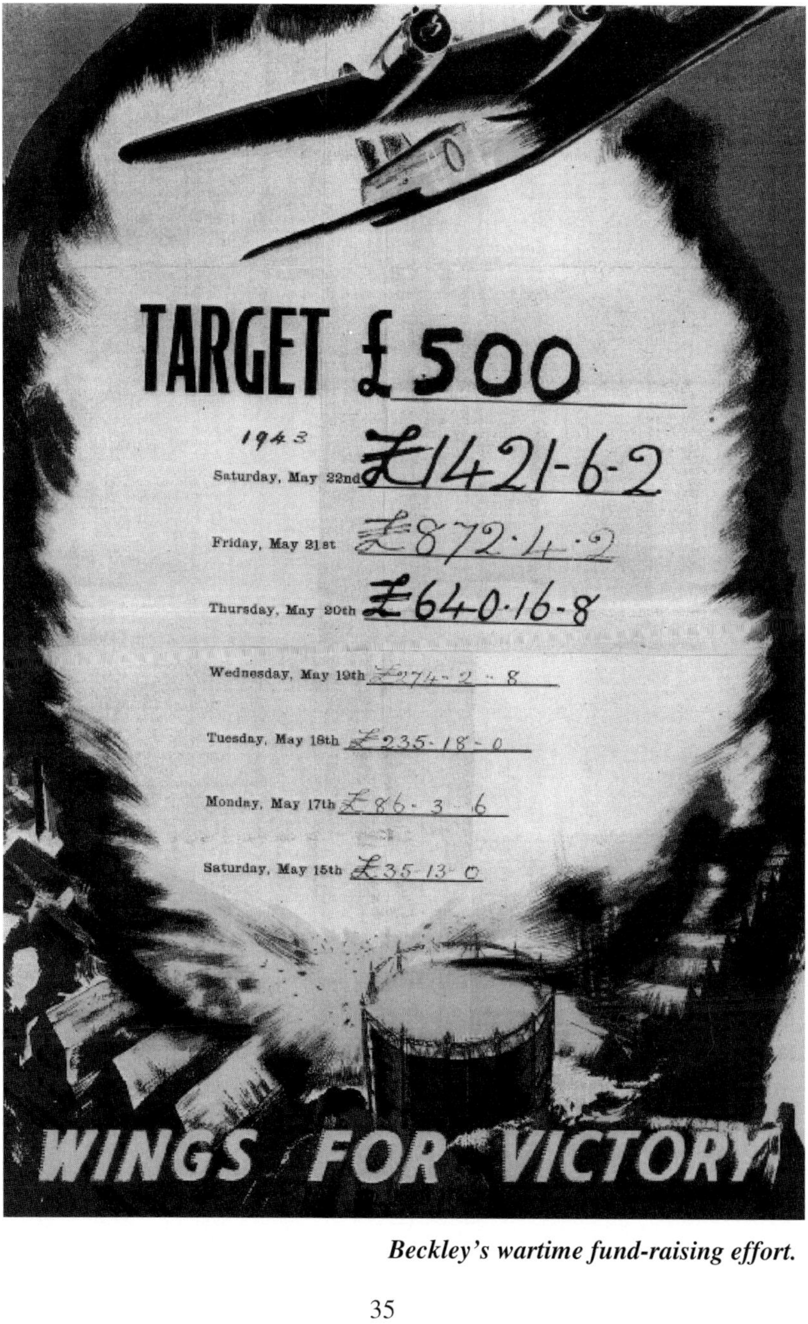

TARGET £500

1943

Saturday, May 22nd £1421-6-2

Friday, May 21st £872·4·2

Thursday, May 20th £640·16·8

Wednesday, May 19th £74·2·8

Tuesday, May 18th £235·18·0

Monday, May 17th £86·3·6

Saturday, May 15th £35·13·0

WINGS FOR VICTORY

Beckley's wartime fund-raising effort.

a United States Air Force aeroplane had dropped the bomb which was then denied. It was somewhat significant however, that the following morning the site was visited by several USAF officers with lots of gold braid on their uniforms. Strangely, the type of bomb dropped had never been used before for practice on the moor, and the Americans usually preferred to bomb in daylight. Could it have been that the bomb was never intended to be dropped on Otmoor?

In his book 'One Wing High', Harry Lomas a wartime Royal Air Force navigator, mentions flying on bombing practice in Wellington bombers to drop 25lb bombs on a range near Oxford, undoubtedly Otmoor. Operating from an airfield at Moreton in the Marsh, he points out the wide differences in results, from excellent - within 20 yards of the target, to one of 2000 yards plus, caused by the bomb spinning violently as it left the aircraft.

With so many airfields in close proximity to the village (there being over a hundred within a few minutes flying time away), inevitably it was in the air that the impact of war was most felt. Apart from the bombing range which was in continuous use, the skies were constantly full of aircraft, and some accidents occurred. Early in the war a Hampden bomber on a practice run across the moor, suddenly nose-dived to earth at the side of Fencott bridge. Later a twin boom P38 Lockheed Lightning exploded and broke up towards Brill, causing one village youngster to say "Its lock has broken".

On the afternoon of 13th November 1940, villagers witnessed a German Junkers 88 bomber with smoke pouring from one of its engines, flying low over the moor and struggling to gain height up over the village, closely followed by two Spitfire fighters. It had apparently been spotted by the fighters over Coventry, they then chased the bomber across country passing immediately over Beckley. A few minutes later it crash-landed on the Downs at Woodwains Farm near Blewbury (at that time in Berkshire), and was subsequently put on display in front of St John's College in St Giles, Oxford as part of a war fund raising venture. The pilot Feldwebel Willi Erwin was captured together with two of his crew, one other crewman having been killed by gunfire. The victory was credited jointly to the Spitfire pilots, Flight Lieutenant Leather and Pilot Officer Johnson belonging to 611 squadron .

Later in the war the skies reverberated to the morale lifting sounds of Lancasters, Wellingtons and Whitley bombers departing on the 'thousand bomber raids', massed in formation American Flying Fortresses going on daylight raids, Stirling's, Halifax's and Dakota's, with white painted bands on their wings, either loaded with parachutists or towing gliders; all on their way, first to the D day landings in Normandy, and later to Arnhem and the Rhine crossings. We also saw the low flying Lancasters, the "Dambusters" (although we didn't know who they were or where they were going at the time) on their way to bomb the Möehne, Sorpe and Eder dams in Germany. To train they used a route around the country resembling the way they would take into their targets, and the Cotswolds were very like the Ruhr hills. They flew so low it was frightening when they came over and it was not unusual for the aircraft to pick up quite large tree branches.

In 1942, a big army exercise was held in this area, for two weeks we were practically under siege, with soldiers, tanks and guns everywhere. Grove Farm was the headquarters of the Royal Ulster Rifles with the cookhouse in the end of the barn, (now a house, Grove Barn). Every ditch and fold in the ground seemed to be occupied by troops ready to repulse the 'enemy'. Crusader and Valentine tanks and Bren gun carriers played havoc with fields of standing crops and hedgerows, it was exciting but also very dangerous to walk on most of the areas roads as a tank could burst through the hedge at any time. At that time there was a wide grass verge in front of Stowood, between Royal Oak and Lodge Farms. This verge was littered with several burnt out tanks and abandoned equipment including live ammunition.

Rationing became very severe and shortages in most things was quite common. Probably country dwellers were fortunate that most of them were able to keep chickens and pigs and grow sufficient vegetables for their needs. In the days before refrigerators became available, when a pig was killed the fresh meat was distributed around family, friends and neighbours, a practice that was reciprocated when they in turn killed their pigs. Every part of the animal was used, The joints not distributed were salted, the sides and hams were marinated in treacle, stout, cider etc, when it was available, every one having their own favourite recipe. Brawn was made from the head and trotters and lard rendered from the fatty flear. A story circulated that a well known local butcher whilst on a pig killing visit was driving between Beckley and Horton when a large deer jumped out of Blackwater Wood and lay stunned in the road after hitting the side of the van. 'H' quickly grabbed his butchers tools from the back and many local families subsequently enjoyed 'off the ration' venison

The eventual cessation of hostilities in 1945 brought about a general reduction in air activity, but for the villagers of Beckley and the six other Otmoor towns, the sounds of war continued unabated. The continuing "Cold War" meant that the bombing range remained in constant use until the late 1950's. Now all these years later in the 1990's, the RAF and Luftwaffe's legacy of unexploded bombs are still being dug up on Otmoor.

An Eastender Remembers   by Len Ferris

I was an evacuee from Holborn to Beckley in 1939. Although parting from my family was emotionally quite upsetting, being thirteen years of age it was probably not so bad for me as many of the others who were much younger. After being deposited at the school we were allocated to our new homes, mine being one of the bungalows in what I believe is now called Bungalow Close. I was reasonably comfortable there but could not understand why potatoes, swedes and carrots were stored under my bed. I was expected to take my foster parents baby for walks in a pram, which gave me a good idea of the layout of the village. I was given a bicycle and went to school at Stanton-St-John. My younger sister was sent to Upper Park Farm and hated it, she could not accept country life at all! After absconding and making her way back to London several times, it was decided she could stay at home there.

After a while I went to live with the Atkins family who lived in the house at Church Corner, now High Corner House. Mr Atkins was head-gardener at Grove House. During the London Blitz my family suffered very badly, our home was bombed, my elder brother was killed and my father sustained injuries from which he subsequently died.

Len Ferris

39

Beckley High Street approx 1930's

High Street junction with Otmoor Lane early 1900's

Chapter Four

Otmoor, or Otta's Fen

Once again we have a dilemma, Otmoor was originally known as Otta's Fen, we do not know who or what Otta was. He, (or even perhaps she?) has faded into the mists of time, leaving only our imagination to provide an answer. I prefer to think of **him** as an ancient local character.

Over the centuries Beckley has been very closely associated with 'The Moor'. From Roman times when the only road ever to cross it was built by them, to the latter half of the 20th century when the moor had become, due to a massive draining enterprise, a place where crops could be grown successfully for the first time in living memory. Now, due to efforts by the Royal Society for the Protection of Birds, a large part of it is to be returned to its earlier wet state to encourage the birds who disappeared when the drainage was carried out, to come back. Otmoor and its 'Seven Towns' has also in the past, been a hotbed of dissension and revolt.

For years the moor was a lonely desolate place, inhabited only by the birds. The absence of other than

41

primitive drainage, meant that from November to March every year, the whole area was under one or two feet of water. During the rest of the year the area was still very boggy. In consequence it was difficult to grow crops, other than hay, although the commoners of Otmoor used the rough grazing for their sheep, cattle and fowls during the better seasons of the year.

There is a theory however, that the moor was not always so wet. There is evidence of ancient ridge and furrow cultivation and of wheat, barley, beans and hay being grown in the early 17th century. In the latter part of the century, there was a series of earthquakes in the area that could have lowered the moor by several feet, which meant that the river Ray and the streams feeding it were more likely to flood.

Going back to Norman times the inhabitants of the seven Otmoor towns of Beckley, Horton, Noke, Charlton, Oddington, Fencott and Murcott had common rights of use on the moor to graze their animals, whereas the fowlery and fishery rights were held by the Lord of the Manor of Beckley. There were strict rules governing the usage of the land, regarding the numbers of animals and the time of year they could be 'turned out'.

The rules were enforced by a Moor Court consisting of twelve moormen, two from each of the larger towns and one from Fencott and one from Murcott. The Court imposed fines on commoners who broke the rules, and impounded animals found on the moor that did not belong to genuine Otmoor inhabitants. Apparently the pound was where Pound Cottage in Beckley High Street is now, although there was also a small pound that used to be alongside Shipley Cottage. The animals were branded with the first letter of their town of origin, the branding irons being kept at Beckley. I wonder how the individual owners sorted out their animals? Cattle on the moor were susceptible to a wasting disease called 'Moor Evil' which was probably an early form of Foot and Mouth disease.

The following is a list of one time members of the Moor Court:-

Beckley: Thomas Mayowe, Johannes Burnham.
Charleton: John Kirby, Henry Poole.
Horton: William Ledwell, William Ply.
Odington: Richard Lambe, Thomas Newell.
Murcott: Thomas Wiatt.
Noke: Jo Mercer, Jo Quartermayne.
Fencott: Peter Kirby.

Notice the old English spellings of Charlton and Oddington.

The Enclosure Acts of the 19th century, sparked off the Otmoor riots, although as early as 1787 when moves were afoot for an Act of Enclosure, the Earl of Abingdon then opposed and defeated plans to secure the Parliamentary Bill. He was supported at that time by the representatives of 340 families from the Otmoor villages. In 1801 George, Duke of Marlborough petitioned Parliament to drain and partition 4000 acres between the seven Otmoor parishes. Notices of intention were supposed to be displayed on church doors, but due to the belligerent threats of the inhabitants of several villages, this was only carried out at Noke. There followed an extensive investigation into the history of Otmoor, but no record could be found of any rights of common use, or indeed of any Lord of the Manor ever having absolute rights. It was then decided that the agreements must have been verbal, so therefore, presumably, could be ignored! A new application was then

£100 Reward

AND

PARDON.

WHEREAS it hath been represented to His Majesty's Government that the Laws have been violated by maliciously disposed Persons conspiring together, and riotously and tumultuously assembling by Night and cutting the Fences and destroying the Bridges on

OTMOOR,

whereby serious injury has been done to the Property, and the Peace of the Neighbourhood has been disturbed;—Now, in order to discover and bring to justice the Offenders,

A REWARD OF

One Hundred Pounds

is hereby offered to any Person who shall give such information to any of His Majesty's Justices of the Peace for the County of Oxford as shall lead to the conviction of any Person or Persons upon any Indictment that may be preferred against him or them for having actually committed any of the crimes of

Felony, Riot, or Conspiracy,

upon the Moor, or for having instigated or encouraged the commission of any of those Crimes either by Words, or by giving Money or Beer.

And, as a further encouragement, HIS MAJESTY'S

FREE PARDON

is hereby promised to any Person giving such information.

By order of His Majesty's Secretary of State for the Home Department.

Whitehall, March 2, 1833.

A copy of a poster dated 1833. This was when the disturbances over the enclosure of Otmoor were still going on, and the offers, worth a fortune to the poor commoners no doubt helped to bring about an early end to the riots. Reproduced by kind permission of Oxfordshire Archives.

made in 1814, and despite vigorous protests from the inhabitants of the villages, became law in July 1815. Drainage and fencing was started immediately. Popular opinion at the time was that the men considered to be mainly responsible for the enclosures were, Sir Alexander Croke, of Horton cum Studley, J.Sawyer Esq. who owned land at Oddington and Charlton, the Rev.P.Serle, Rector of Oddington, and the Rev. T.L.Cooke,Vicar of Beckley.

The passing of the act meant that the poorer inhabitants could only keep their long established rights of commonage by paying a share of the costs incurred in draining and fencing, this was of course way beyond their means. The effect on the families whose income and access to sources of food for themselves and their animals were severely reduced, was little short of disastrous. Surely, a classic example of Percy Bysshe Shelley's words, "The rich have become richer, and the poor have become poorer."

As the years went by, resentment festered and flared. Drainage dykes and ditches were breached, fences, gates and bridges torn down and smashed. The Oxfordshire Militia were called out on frequent occasions to restore order, and in 1830 several wagon loads of moormen who had been arrested were being taken to Oxford Prison. It was the annual St Giles' Fair and when they reached Beaumont Street, the crowds attending the Fair attacked the soldiers and all the prisoners were set free. The disturbances continued for several years, only dying down following offers of rewards and pardons for information leading to the conviction of the dissidents. I imagine that the sums offered, worth a fortune then to the poor commoners, would have been very hard to resist even when it meant the betrayal of ones neighbours.

Probably the only consolation the moormen of the Seven Towns had for their loss of common usage, was the fact that the land, despite many attempts at drainage, remained very marshy, and did not fulfil the expectations of value for the new landowners.

An old rhyme supposedly written locally at the time shrewdly sums up the whole Enclosure situation:-

The fault is great in Man or Woman
Who steals the Goose from off a common
But who can plead that man's excuse
Who steals the Common from the Goose ?

The moor continued to flood extensively every winter and in 1887 a baby Newell had to be transported from Lower Woods Farm for his christening in Beckley Church, part of the way by boat, during which his grandmother lost her best bonnet in the flood waters. Apparently 1904 and 1908 were years when the floods were particularly high.

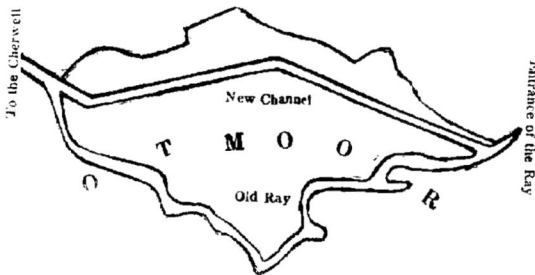

Plan for Diverting the River Ray from 'The Case Of Otmoor With The Moor Orders' by Sir Alexander Croke 1831.

Quieter Times ?

During the period from the 1930s to the late 50s, the moor was used by the Royal Air Force as a bombing range, and in 1953 until the present day, the eastern part of it by the Army, as a firing range.

In the years following the departure of the RAF, an extensive drainage scheme was undertaken in the central and western parts of the moor. Large dykes and banks were excavated and electric pumping stations installed. In consequence cereal crops were grown on the valley floor successfully for the first time in living memory. Unfortunately many hedgerows were grubbed out, removing much of the habitat for wildlife.

The numbers of birds both native and migratory that inhabited the moor before, and during the second world war, was probably uncountable, very different when following the drainage, on the western side, often the number of birds seen or even heard could be counted on one hand. It is hoped that this situation will improve over the coming years, when the proposed new nature reserve becomes established. In 1996 The Royal Society for the Protection of Birds obtained over 520 acres (220 hectares) and subsequently in 1998 another 128 acres (52 hectares) of arable field which are being restored to wetlands and reedbeds. Eventually it is hoped that many of the dozens of species of birds that frequented the moor will return. High water levels will be maintained throughout the winter to attract a range of wildfowl and wading birds. In spring the water levels will recede but the soil will remain damp for the

benefit of breeding waders such as snipe, redshank, lapwing and curlew. Once the reedbed is established it is hoped that bitterns will colonise along with water rails, reed warblers and bearded tits. In summer once the breeding season is over, the grasslands will be cut for hay or grazed by cattle and possibly sheep, brought to the reserve by local farmers. The work commenced in 1997 with a three year major works programme, followed hopefully, by the return of the birds. Use will be made of the existing pumping stations, but by reversing the process and retaining the water, not pumping it out.

Lapwing

The following paragraph is an extract from an RSPB Newsletter in April 1998:-

"Ironically, the contractors carrying out the work to create the new reedbed were employed by local farmers to drain the land over 20 years ago. Some of the men working for White Horse Contractors are now undoing their original work."

Beckley Parish Council and many residents have expressed concern at the implication of many sightseers in cars passing through the village to view the birds. Traffic is bound to increase and it is difficult to see how, despite assurances from the RSPB, it will be possible to control in the future .

The land taken over by the RSPB will adjoin some 500 acres (210 hectares) on the eastern side of the moor owned by the Ministry of Defence, which has largely escaped the use of intensive modern farming methods. As a result of the absence

48

of inorganic fertilisers, herbicides and
pesticides, the land was first notified as a
Site of Special Scientific Interest (SSSI)
in 1952 and re-notified under the 1981
Wildlife and Countryside Act in 1988. As
with other MOD properties, Otmoor has
an active conservation group led up to

Snipe

1998 by the Assistant Secretary for the TAVRA, (Territorial,
Auxiliary and Volunteer Reserve Association) with
representatives from English Nature (which oversees
management via its SSSI consultation procedures). The
County Naturalist's Trust, BBONT (Berkshire,
Buckinghamshire and Oxfordshire Naturalist's Trust, which
has an access agreement over the southern part.), The
Environment Agency (which undertakes ditch maintenance
works.), The Oxford Ornithological Society (which
undertakes bird recording.) and Pond Action (which advises
on pond creation), Other people and organisations are co-
opted as matters arise. The group has contributed to the
conservation section of the TAVRA's management plan for
the moor, as part of the MOD's national aim to have
management plans operating on all its land holdings. MOD's
purpose is to have due consideration paid to the nature
conservation interest, and this aim has been formalised within
the Declaration of Intent signed by the Ministry of Defence
and English Nature in 1992. Through this partnership, a large
number of works have been, or are planned to be, undertaken
to safeguard and enhance this nationally important site.

Open water habitats are well represented on the eastern
side of Otmoor with a number of shallow pools and a network
of ditches. The ditches are often independent of surrounding
land and, in the absence of nitrate and phosphate pollutants,

they contain very pure water. In addition, the area regularly floods in winter encouraging over-wintering of wildfowl and waders. Being clay based, Otmoor is dependent on this winter flooding, together with the general cycle of rainfall. Without it the wetland habitats and open water would dry out and lose most of its interest.

Otmoor is rich in water plants. The ditches contain branched bur-weed, reed sweet-grass, greater reedmace, water plantain and flowering rush. Many contain rare plants like arrowhead, frogbit, and fat and ivy-leafed duckweeds. The large central pool, known as 'Fowl Pill', is particularly rich in uncommon plants, including water violet and bladderwort.

In 1991 an extension to Fowl Pill was constructed together with some experimental pools. The work was undertaken by the then National Rivers Authority, (Now the Environment Agency) aided by Pond Action. The purpose was to increase the area of open water on Otmoor and encourage more wetland wildlife in particular, it aims to provide additional feeding areas for wading birds and their chicks in the breeding season March to July inclusive. Birds such as snipe need soft, muddy areas to enable the chicks to feed; without such areas many will inevitably starve to death.

In 1997 scrub clearance caused some inevitable soil disturbance. As a result, the naturalists were delighted to see

Viola persicifolia

50

the re-emergence of the Fen Violet *Viola persicifolia*. A rare plant that had not been seen on Otmoor since 1962. There are only two other sites remaining where the Fen Violet is found, they are Woodwalton Fen and Wicken Fen in Cambridgeshire. Work is taking place to ensure that the plant is not lost again. Seed has been collected and sent to the Kew seed bank and the Oxford University Botanical Garden. Plans are in hand to include suitable management of the site in future, and it is hoped that the Fen Violet will appear or be introduced on the adjacent RSPB site. The future of this rare species now looks a good deal more secure than was once thought.

Two species of butterfly are of particular importance to nature conservation on Otmoor because of their national status as rare and declining species, they are, the Marsh Fritillary and the Black Hairsreak. The Marsh Fritillary, *Eurodryus aurinia*, was once found all over Great

Marsh Fritillary

Britain, but has declined severely since the 1940's. It is now extinct in eastern Britain with the most easterly colony surviving on Otmoor. The life cycle of this butterfly is carried out on a perennial plant found in damp meadows and calcareous grassland, the Devil's-bit Scabious. The Black Hairstreak, *Strymonidia pruni*, is confined to the wooded clay belt running through Oxon, Beds, Cambs and Northants. Most colonies are small consisting at most of a few hundred adults, although even less are seen due to their habit of perching in tree tops. This butterfly needs high densities of blackthorn or wild plum growing in sunny sheltered situations. Whilst this type of habitat is very prevalent in England, the butterfly's restricted distribution is probably due to its sedentary behaviour in rarely leaving its small foraging areas. On Otmoor, rotational coppice-work of the blackthorn hedgerows is carried out. This has the effect of providing a continuous supply of suitable blackthorn for egg-laying; and preventing enroachment of the hedges into the adjacent species-rich grassland, which is the home of the marsh fritillary as well as all the other plants and animals.

With the existence of a firing range on the site, it seems a contradiction to have weapons of war and wildlife prospering side by side, but the MOD must be congratulated and thanked for their foresight and active custodianship of the flora and fauna of Otmoor. There surely cannot be a sweeter sound, than to stand on the range, at dusk, on a still summer evening, and listen to the nightingales singing in Horton Spinney, long may they continue to do so. It is also significant that during all the years the moor was used for bombing practice, the birds were never frightened away, always being present in large numbers. It is only since the advent of drainage and intensive farming that they have all but disappeared.

From the 1960's through to the 1980's the moor was under the threat of having a motorway built across it. Also the Water Board resurrected a plan to flood the area for a reservoir. The ecological and social disasters that could have followed from the implementation of any of these schemes were thankfully averted and the story of the battles fought against them can be found in another section of this journal.

Otmoor range was, until the defence review of 1998, provided and managed by Eastern Wessex Territorial Auxiliary and Volunteer Reserve Association (TAVRA) for the development of skill at arms vital to the training of Reserve and Regular Forces, and target shooting by Cadet Forces. Through national agreements, it is also used by Police Forces and others. Now it is understood that control of the range is passing from the TAVRA to Southern Command of the regular army, and rumours abound as to their intentions for the future of the site. Whatever happens it is hoped that the valuable conservation work carried out previously will still be ongoing by the new administrators.

The 8-lane Gallery range, with firing points from 100 to 600 yards, serves units in the Thames Valley and adjacent counties. It is active from 0930 -1600 hrs each Monday, Wednesday and Friday, and at weekends throughout the year; also from 1730-2000 hrs during the summer months on some Mondays, Wednesdays and Fridays.

A red masthead flag flown at the STOP BUTT, together with red boundary flags at key access points around the moor, indicate that the RANGE IS ACTIVE AND MUST NOT BE ENTERED. A flashing light on the Stop Butt may be used in place of the boundary flags when access to the flags is not possible due to flooding -the RED FLAG on the Stop Butt will always be flown.

Access to Otmoor is provided by a number of public footpaths and bridleways whenever the range is closed, (usually Tuesdays and Thursdays, and before and after firing). Further access can also be arranged either by contacting BBONT (01865-775476), the Range Warden (01865-358995) or the RSPB (01295-253330) Information boards setting out the Bylaws, range danger area warning signs, and routes of rights of way are sited at all access points.

How fortunate we are to have such a legacy of social and natural history that is Otmoor, and right on our doorstep, the future surely holds much promise. However, we must continue to be vigilant against whatever future threats that might arise, and be prepared to fight against so called 'progress' as did our predecessors the 'Otmoor Commoners', albeit unsuccessfully, against money and influence, all those years ago - but the spirit was there!

Another view of the Joseph Stone By Simon Hogg

Around the year 1817, an unknown artist produced a number of drawings of local buildings which he followed up with very accurate paintings of the same scenes. Because of the accuracy with which he recorded what he saw, I see no reason why he should suddenly use poetic licence with his drawing and painting of the Joseph Stone in the middle of Otmoor.

In his day the stone was very much larger than is shown in the photograph taken by Miss Morley and published in the booklet 'Otmoor and its Seven Towns', where one reads that it was later broken into two pieces and as we all know it has been crumbling away ever since.

Various suggestions as to its use have been made including, a Roman milestone, an ancient surveyors mark stone and of course a mounting stone to help you up when you are down. In addition to these suggestions, I would like to add that due to the stones original size and construction, as shown in the picture, there are two further useful purposes that it must have served. The picture shows a roughly hewn circular stone set on the moors trackside, with two steps around it at different heights.

In bygone days, when the moor used to experience considerable flooding, the stone rising up out of the flood water, would have served as a valuable guide to help you keep to the track when riding on horseback across the moor. The two steps around the stone would have served as a permanent depth gauge, visible from some distance away to show the depth of water at that point.

It seems most unlikely that the stones creator did not see these further uses, in addition to the ones for which it was originally constructed.

The picture of the Joseph Stone resides in the Bodleian Library and its reference is as follows :- MS.Top.Oxon.a.42, fol.28.

Simon C.Hogg. 1994

The Battle of Otmoor fought about 1830
Originally about 4000 acres Tithe, Tax and Rent free!

The heading above and the following poem was written by Richard (Dickie) Coles a Beckley character. He died in 1923 aged 85 years. The words typify the feelings of loss and anger, and eventual hopelessness of the Otmoor commoners brought about by the Act of Enclosure. The poem is reproduced by kind permission of John and Ann Wing who own the manuscript.

Come you men of 'Beckley Town'
And have you heard the story
Of the battle, fought on Otmoor ground
By our fathers now in glory.

The Parsons wanted all the land
The Otmoor folks did grumble,
Then cowhouses they set on fire
And longed to see them tumble.

They said the House an act had, passed
Our Common to enclose
But when they came to. take possession
It was then we came to blows.

These gentry got two hundred men
To make their hedges and ditches,
The Otmoor women left off their clothes
And took to wearing breeches.

Six hundred of them marched out
With pitchforks on their shoulders,
For they had sworn a bitter oath
To slaughter all the soldiers.

The marching out looked very bold
But women are easily scared,
The soldiers all pulled out their swords
And the women stood and stared.

They stood and stared with all their might
Examining the motions,
They could not use their forks at all
They had such funny notions.

There was Beckley on the hill
And Noke in the hole,
The Oddington gals
Are as black as any coal.

Charlton is a pretty place
And Fencott is another
Murcott is a dirty place
And Horton is its brother.

So they parked us in their wagons
To take us for a ride,
They started then for Oxford jail
And the soldiers rode beside.

But when they came to Oxford Town
It was St Giles' Fair,
And many of our countrymen
Were met together there.

With sticks and stones and such like there
They the soldiers did attack,
And they went at it with such will
They soon drove the villains back.

57

Then all at once we were set free
Which made us very glad,
But when the gentry heard of it
It drove them swearing mad.

But when we do fight again
We won't trust to the women,
A soldiers sword will conquer them
And set their heads a swimming.

The people always had enough
For they fed their cattle free,
A happier place in all the land
I am sure there could not be.

But now they are scattered o'er the earth
Some have to New Zealand gone,
And some have took to thieving
And a few at home are grieving.

Richard Coles.

'The Moor' 1936-1996.

The moor was a wild mysterious place
Subject of legend and tales of lore.
No crops grown then, that have been now
On and across the valley floor.

Wild birds there were in plenty
Prospering through the moorland day,
Bewicks and Widgeon, Bittern too
Before the waters were drained away.

Seldom clear and never dry
Wraith like mists would swiftly appear.
Eerie church bells sounding afar
Brought a moment of panic or even of fear.

In childhood days many adventures enjoyed
We could have been in a far off land,
But sodden clothing and soaking feet
Brought parental rebuke by a heavy hand.

The Air Force came and built two towers
Their bomb bursts for to spy,
'Keep clear' they said 'it is not safe'
When the red flags flying high.

Then in the war they lit it up
The Germans for to hoax,
A decoy airfield there was made
The enemy bombs to coax.

The war was over, but the bombs still fell
No peace by night or day,
Until at last we were relieved,
When the bombers flew away.

At last, we thought all will be back
To as it was before,
Alas, it was not meant to be,
They drained the valley floor.

But wait, there is again some hope,
RSPB   the wetlands will restore,
We can look forward to the time
When the birds return once more.

By A Beckley Resident 1996.

Beckley RAF Tower under construction by local labour

Chapter Five

The Church

Introduced by
Rev. Dr. William Brierley Team Vicar

The closing years of the twentieth century have proved to be ones of great change and uncertainty throughout society. This has been felt most acutely in those institutions which have traditionally provided the stable foundations of our nation. Within the Church as a whole, this is very much a time for looking at where we are and seeing how we might step forward into the twenty-first century.

This century has seen Beckley Church change from having its own Vicar, living in the village, to being part of a Team of Twelve Churches and sharing a non-resident Team Vicar with three other parishes. This presents both drawbacks and opportunities: the major drawback being the question of how much time I can spend in the village, and the major opportunity being the greater resources which a larger group of churches can afford. The clearest example of the latter was the appointment of a Youth Minister to the Wheatley Team, to work specifically with young people. This was something which Beckley alone, or even the four parishes, could never have hoped for.

In reflecting upon Beckley Church at this time, it seems to me that its greatest strengths lie in the commitment of its congregation, its tradition of reflective Eucharistic worship and the beauty of its church building. The greatest needs of the church are to incorporate families, young people and children into its life, and to find a more effective means of heating to prevent worshippers from freezing in the winter months. The first of these needs was reflected in the start of a Sunday School in the summer of 1997, and the beginning of a monthly family service in October 1997. My involvement with the village school, as a Governor and in taking weekly assemblies, has also provided invaluable opportunities to restate the church's interest in and support of families and children within the village. In terms of the church heating, the support that I received when I ran the 1997 Otmoor Challenge in aid of the church heating, indicated that the second of the needs was clearly recognised!

I feel very optimistic about Beckley Church. It is firmly rooted and grounded in the traditions of the Christian faith. This is a very rich soil from which to bring forth new growth in the century that lies before us.

Rev. Dr. William Brierley

As it was in the beginning

Very little is known about the first church built on the site other than that it was Saxon and was built of wood. About the year 1150 the little church was pulled down and in its place a new stone church was built in the late Norman style. A section of the Norman north wall of the chancel still survives and forms part of the present church. Though the wall has been pierced by a 19th century flue, it is still clearly distinguishable - windowless and tapering.

No building in the Early English Gothic style of the 13th century is to be found in Beckley Church, but at the very end of the century, in the reign of Edward I, 1272-1307, when the new 'Decorated Gothic' style was just beginning, a very extensive enlargement of the Norman church took place. The Norman chancel was lengthened and enlarged, the old north wall being retained, the Norman nave was pulled down and a large central tower was built in its place, with transepts north and south, and a new nave to the west. This produced a fine cruciform church with chancel and nave of exactly the same length. The central tower was a ' lantern ' - it had no floors, and its upper windows threw a stream of light on to great crucifixion figures on its walls.

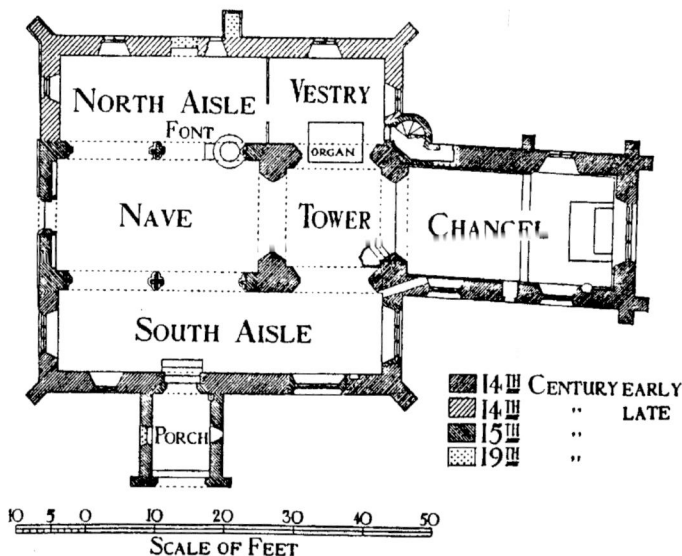

PLAN OF THE CHURCH OF THE ASSUMPTION

The Norman church, was built to face sunrise on August 22nd the octave day of the Feast of Assumption. When the cruciform church was built the new building was made to face sunrise on August 15th - the feast itself. Hence the odd difference of direction between the chancel and the nave - the skew chancel.

Ruth Dawber

Before the transepts had stood a hundred years they were pulled down to make room for a long aisle (wing) on each side of the church. Each aisle had its own high-pitched roof. This work would have been done during the reigns of Henry IV, 1399-1413, and of Henry V,1413-1422.   Although a great deal of work was done in the 15th century, the ground plan of the church was not changed except by the addition of a porch. Inside the church the low nave arches of the previous century were removed and the present lofty ones built instead, with tall pillars all in the beautiful Perpendicular Gothic style. The roofs (except that of the chancel) were flattened and covered with lead, enabling clerestory windows to be inserted high up over the arches. This at once made the nave beautifully light. The south doorway too was rebuilt - it is a very fine example of late Perpendicular work. The ironwork on the inner door is probably a lot older than the door itself.

The font dates from 1200. It stood originally in the nave of the Norman church, and is now in front of a stone carved bookrest, probably made for reading the gospel at Sunday Mass.

The years go by

The parish chest (c.1350) was restored in 1953 at the Victoria and Albert Museum. An interesting extract taken from the Parochial Church records in the 1950's gives the background on the provision of parish chests .

In the time of King Henry II 1154-1189 a royal mandate was issued ordering chests to be placed in all churches. In every church there was to be provided - a hollow trunk fastened with three keys to be kept by the Bishop, the parish priest and a religious layman for money from the faithful for crusades, A further order to provide chests was made by the Synod of Exeter in 1287 - a chest for books and vestments. The poor law of 1552 directed the parishioners to provide a strong chest with a hole in the upper part and having three keys, for holding alms for the poor. The orders were repeated in Elizabethan legislation and made even more definite in the canons of 1603. From time to time over the years suggestions have been made that the Beckley chest be sold to raise money for repairs or improvements in the church. Thankfully it has always been decided that the chest be kept.

There is a squint or hagioscope through the wall so that worshippers in the south aisle could see the priest at the high altar, there was also one now blocked up on the other side where the vestry is now.

The circular turret staircase up to the tower was built in 1420 which presumably was when the floors were built in the tower. An inventory taken in the 1550's indicated that the church had four large bells and a sanctus bell. There are now five bells, two from the 17th, two from the 18th and one from the 19th century and also a sanctus bell. Sadly, all except the small Sanctus (or Priest's) bell are now unable to be rung.

The pulpit is Jacobean (James I. 1603-1625). It originally stood in the nave against the nearer pillar. On the wall alongside is a bracket for holding an hour glass. The hour glass itself was stolen together with the chalice and candle holders in 1982 and never recovered.

In 1788 a gallery was erected for the 'use of singers', this provides a puzzle, where was it put? Apparently the usual place was on the west wall but there is no sign of where it could have been. It was taken down in 1845. There is a blocked up opening high up on the east wall of the nave through from the bell-ringing floor. It was possible that if it was a door it gave access to a rood loft but there is no

Beckley Church Choir date not known but as the Rev. Phillip Doyne is in the picture it was taken during his term of office between 1894-1916

evidence to support this theory. Of course it may just have been a window in the tower or access outside on to the roof before it was raised.

A plaster ceiling was removed at this time so that the 15th century timber roof was exposed. The clock situated on the ringing floor was installed in 1883.

The Stained Glass

There are some rare examples of 14th and 15th century stained glass, in the north aisle are two panels of mediaeval glass c.1350. The left panel shows   St. James the Great (James of Compostella), patron saint of pilgrims, wearing a floppy hat and carrying a scrip (bag) in his hand. To his right is St. Christopher (upper half modern). The figure in the second window to the right (c.1425) represents the education of the Virgin and shows St. Anne teaching Our Lady to read. The small roundel above has the monogram AM for Ave Maria.

Most of the glass in the three windows in the east end is by Hardman of Birmingham (1895). The north window repays study with its symbols of Christ and the Holy Eucharist - the Lamb, the Pelican, the Wheat, the Grapes and the Vine. Together with the scenes of the Last Testament 'types' of the bread from heaven in the wilderness and the priesthood - Melchisedek.

North window; above St Edmund, King and Martyr, who carries arrows in his hand as a reminder of his torture before death at the hand of the Danes in 870(c.1325-50). The centre of his cult was at Bury St. Edmunds, Suffolk.

East window; the left quatrefoil, the coronation of the Virgin. Christ places the crown on the Virgins head. Neither figure has a nimbus. The right quatrefoil shows the assumption of the Virgin and St. Thomas receiving her girdle. This panel is unusual in the reclining position of the Virgin, as she is carried upward by the angels. She herself hands down the girdle to St. Thomas, instead of standing upright with the girdle falling from her. Above is the blessing hand of God, (Manus Dei,) while St. Thomas kneels by the empty tomb (c.1325-50). Over the past years these panels have had expert conservation treatment. In 1987/88 they were lent to the Royal Academy of Arts for the 'Age of Chivalry' exhibition.

South window; the Assumption of the Virgin. Our Lady in a mandorla is carried up by four angels, with two censing angels above (c.1300-10).

Wall Paintings

There are many wall paintings, that through careful restoration work have been uncovered.

In the Lady Chapel, South Aisle, above the parish chest are mediaeval wall paintings, late 13th or 14th century. In the centre, Our Lady suckling the Christ Child. Above a weighing of souls, St. Michael holds a balance in his hands. Our Lady stands on the right, her prayers symbolised by her rosary which she places in the pan of the scales. To the left a figure of a devil tries to pull the scale in his favour. Above the

Torments of the Damned. A body is roasting on a spit, the flames fanned by bellows, the body basted by a devilish figure above. To the left, the next victim awaits its turn, hanging by the feet from a meat-hook. To the left again, is the remains of a later and larger (15th century) Weighing of Souls which covered much of the wall. Only the left pan of the scales remains. The white strip of plaster may indicate the position of an earlier screen. An indecipherable inscription runs at the top of these paintings.

In the nave, the tower wall is covered by a faint, but in its main features largely complete, painting of the Last Judgement - known sometimes as a Doom - from the 15th century. Christ sits in majesty, supported by Our Lady St. Mary (left) and St. John the Baptist (right) interceding. The souls of the departed, represented by little naked figures, rise from their tombs - the saved enter the gate of heaven (left) while the damned are consigned to the jaws of hell (right). On the right of the painting is the devil with his catch in a net.

Below the painting of the Last Judgement on the left, is the figure of St. Peter, who carries the papal staff and his emblem of the keys. On the right is St. Paul, who holds a sword and a book. Near the base of the arch on the left is another figure looking up, possibly the donor. These figures appear to be 14th century.

On the west wall are the latest of the paintings to be uncovered. The following is a copy of an article by Anthony de Vere who was vicar of our parish from 1971 until 1994 and who was responsible for all the valuable conservation work carried out during those years :-

Following the break with Rome in 1534 by Henry VIII, 1509 -1547, when the King became the Supreme Head on Earth of the Church of England, The Royal Arms were commonly hung, carved or painted over the chancel arch - or in place of the rood loft. The survival of these in parish churches is not uncommon. The Arms that are to be seen in Beckley church are those of George III who acceded to the throne in 1760.

The survival of other Royal Iconography as wall paintings is much more rare. That is why what we have in Beckley is of special interest. Here we have on the west wall of the nave three sets of Prince of Wales feathers, arranged over the apex of the window and on either side. Those to be seen on the left of the window are composed of three feathers ,the outside two red and the centre one yellow, encircled by a coronet with a jewelled band. This is surmounted by a crown, with the letters H and P on either side. These refer to Henry, Prince of Wales, b.1594, son of James I. He died from typhoid fever in 1612, thus making way for his younger brother, the future Charles I, to become king.

It is interesting to note that the conservators, The Perry Lithgow Partnership (of Chipping Norton) commented that "other examples of Prince of Wales feathers are unknown to me". Part of what is written here is based on their report.

Below the feathers on either side there are scrolls which zigzag down the walls. That on the left has the words "Feare God, Honour the King. Pet i : ii :17."
The scroll on the right has the date 1607 together with the word 'Norris.' It is tempting to think that this might be the name Norreys who owned the manor of Beckley in 1607. He

was Francis Norreys, later Viscount Thame and Earl of Berkshire, who committed suicide with a crossbow in 1623.

Below is a biblical text. The words are adapted from Jeremiah verse two in the Geneva version of 1557. It reads :- "Return ye everyone from his evil ways, make your wages and your workes good. If this nation, against whom I have pronounced, turn from this wickednesse, I will repent of the plague I thought to bring upon them."

Anthony de Vere.

And so to the 20th century

Apart from the conservation work carried out on the

Church Corner around 1900.
It has not changed very much except the elms are now gone and then there were no parked cars !

wall paintings and to the stained glass other more recent alterations and additions are :-

The purchase and installation of the organ. Funding was started in 1928. In 1933 a second hand organ had been seen costing about £125 and £40 to move and install it. The PCC proposed that an offer of £80 be made for the organ with the possibility of going up to £100. No further mention of the organ was made in the PCC minutes, but memory says that it was installed in 1934. An electric pump replacing the hand pumping arrangement was installed in 1962. Previous to the new organ being installed a harmonium type was used, situated just inside the south door. The screen forming the vestry was put up by my father in 1934, using surplus panels from the organ installation.

The church was first wired for electric lighting in 1937 following the coming of the electricity supply to the village. A complete rewire with a new lighting scheme was installed in 1992.

The original heating scheme, probably early Victorian, was by means of a furnace situated in a stokehold near the tower staircase. A series of ducts ran under the floor carrying warm air to large grilles situated around the church. This scheme was then replaced by individual 'tortoise' type stoves, which when going well glowed red and gave off great heat. If you were sitting near to one of the stoves the side nearest the heat was roasted, but frozen on the other, there were also noxious fumes blown out from the heaters when the wind was in a certain direction. The electrical wiring was extended in 1962 with outlets for 3 kilowatt convector heaters, it was still not a satisfactory system, but never the less they remained in use until 1992. At that time Six - 6 kilowatt storage fan heaters were installed, designed to give a continuous low background temperature for fabric preservation. The fans are designed to boost the heating when the church is in use. Small additional heaters were installed in the two central pew blocks in 1998. As with all buildings with high ceilings however, any heating scheme which could provide comfortable temperatures would be prohibitively expensive both to install and run, and is unfortunately beyond the means of our parish, and indeed most other parishes.

In 1982 an area for the burial of ashes was designated on the north side of the church. On the wall above is a tablet in Hopton Wood stone, with lettering by Nicholette Gray. Inside the church, on the west wall to the left of the door is a framed commemorative panel on which are inscribed the names of those whose ashes are interred in the churchyard.

The new central altar, the credence table and the re-ordering scheme under the central tower was carried out in 1986, and was designed by Miss Sheila Gibson F.S.A. The altar rails together with the pierced panels inserted in the altar, are by Augustus Welby Pugin The celebrated Victorian Architect (1812 - 1852). The new stone altar and raised floor in the Lady Chapel South Aisle, was carried out at the same time as the central altar. The icon of the Crucifixion over the altar was painted in 1989 by Mme Nadege Valon in Paris.

Part of the North Aisle was redesigned in 1997 to form "Kate's Corner" in memory of Miss Kate Lea, Academic and former Churchwarden who died in 1995. The work consists of a memorial plaque by carver Paul Wherle, placed in the alcove of the old doorway in the north aisle. A triptych was commissioned from the Horton-cum-Studley artist, Nicholas

Mynheer, to be fixed to the vestry screen. The screen was painted in a shade to compliment the triptych and the floor lightened and polished. The result has improved this side of the church resulting in a vibrant colourful corner.

A description of the Triptych by the artist

The left hand panel depicts the annunciation of the angel to Mary. Not in this case however, to foretell the birth of Christ, but rather to foretell her death. Legend states that after the crucifixion of Christ, Mary lived with the apostle John. In her loneliness she prayed to be delivered from life. An angel appeared to her

Triptych left hand panel

promising that within three days she would enter paradise, where her son awaited her. The angel presented Mary with a palm branch which she handed to St John to be borne before her at her burial.

Triptych right hand panel

The far right panel carries on the legend with the dormition (or death) of the Virgin. At her request the apostles are present at her death. St John is seen holding the palm branch, the symbol of victory (over death). Jesus appears and receives the soul of his mother into heaven.

Finally, the centre panel, The Assumption. After three days Jesus decrees that the soul of his mother should be reunited with her body and that both should be transported to heaven. Mary stands on a crescent moon : the sun and moon being symbols associated with the Blessed Virgin, referring to the 'woman clothed with the sun, and the moon under her feet' (Rev. 12 : 1). She has become the 'Queen of Heaven' and in Art is traditionally portrayed standing on a crescent moon.

Throughout the triptych Earth is represented by cool blue/greens whilst Heaven is warm red, yellow and gold. The gold, symbolic of the Divine, ties Earth to Heaven in each panel. The bands of gold arch inwards and upwards to the top of the central panel, to Heaven itself, and God the Father, surrounded by the Heavenly Host, looks down upon all.

Nicholas Mynheer
April 1997.

In an article in the Church Times on the 6th of June 1997, Richard Davey wrote "The commission of the tryptych from Mynheer is a bold and exciting one, which will enhance and enrich Beckley Church for generations to come".

Triptych centre panel

Due to fears of the churchyard becoming overfull, discussions about obtaining extra burial ground were first raised in August 1932. The first option was ground at the north end of the churchyard, then used by the school as a garden, now the driveway to St. Mary's Cottage and Nokewood House. Mrs Cooke the owner, was against using this piece of land because it was not big enough and she did not like the idea of encroaching on the school yard. A piece of 'Home Close', the field at the bottom of Church Street, opposite Mr Coppards cottage (now Meadow Cottage) was suggested. Mrs Cooke did not seem to object to this proposal, so it was decided to ask the Medical Officer of Health to inspect the site. Mrs Cooke however, then decided that the site was not suitable. The end of 1936 saw the negotiations at deadlock.

In 1943 the matter was raised again, Canon Archibald Swainson, the then incumbent, said that he had been told that in municipal cemeteries it was usual for the ground to be re-used after fifteen years, unless it had been bought out. He pointed out that with only three or four funerals a year, a large part of the churchyard had not been used for probably a hundred years or more and there could be no good reason for not using that ground again. Since then the matter has been discussed several times. and now many years later a new site is again being sought. Meanwhile room is still being found in our churchyard .

To commemorate the fifty years since the end of World War Two, the Parish Council decided to plant a Remembrance Tree. After consultations with the Local Authority and the Parochial Church Council, a golden yew was ceremonially planted in the churchyard on Remembrance Sunday, November 12th 1995.

Beckley Parish Church is known as the Church of the Assumption of the Blessed Virgin Mary. The title is in itself unusual as there are very few English churches with this dedication. Anthony de Vere a previous incumbent of this parish, summed up the meaning of the title in an article published in the Beckley Newsletter in 1993 :-
"In a journal I receive from a monastery in

Normandy there is a section which records those of their friends who have died over previous months. They refer to them as "Retourne a Dieu", which I take to mean "returned to God". That, I think, is as good an explanation as I can give of the name or dedication of our village church, The Assumption of the Blessed Virgin Mary. The title speaks of her ' return to God' after the completion of her earthly life. As the hope and expectation of every Christian is to see God, to be with God, it would seem to be a most excellent dedication for a church. The feast of the Assumption of the Blessed Virgin Mary has remained in the Kalendar of the University of Oxford since the time of the Reformation, It is on the 15th of August."

Anthony de Vere

A list of incumbents of this parish.

1230 Nicholas de Anna.
1290 Philip de Heddleshovre.
1298 Henry de Exon.
1301 Jacob de Berkhamstead.
1316 Robert de Handlo
1318 Edmund de Lodelaw.
No records available.
1538 Rogerus Ingram.
1550 John Harwood.
1552 Richard Joyner.
1555 Thomas Hancke.
1557 John Blowne.
1564 John Foxley.
1618 Peter Norcott.
1637 Francis Goddard. (or Goddiar).
1679 Robert Hawkins.
1752 John Baker. B.D.
1764 Gilbert Stephens. LL.D.
1773 Richardson Wood. M.A.
1798 Theophilus Leigh Cooke. M.A.

1847 George Theophilus Cooke. M.A.
1894 Philip Valentine Doyne. M.A.
1916 John Kinchen Smith. M.A.
1932 Edgar Leopold Millen. M.A.
1936 Benjamin Fairthorne Betteridge.
1937 John Copley Winslow. M.A.
1939 Archibald Douglas Swainson. B.A.
1955 A.C.Jarvis. M.A.
1959 Hugh Gilpin Benson. M.A.
1971 Anthony de Vere. M.A.

With the inception of the Team Ministry, the priest is no longer an Incumbent, but is now Team Vicar or the Priest in Charge

1997   William David Brierley.B.A. D.Phil.

Beckley Church Clock   by Simon Hogg

On the occasions when you walk through Beckley you may see or hear the Church clock strike the hour and wonder perhaps who its maker was and what his past history might have been.

The clock was fitted into the church tower in 1883 and is enclosed behind a wooden casing with two doors, which when opened reveals the clocks beautifully shaped, curved cast iron plates, painted

79

maroon with gold letters on the back plate which read:-
'BAILEY ALBION WORKS. SALFORD MANCHESTER.'

The clock was made by one William Bailey who was the son of John Bailey who founded the Albion Works in 1839. In 1886 William aged 28 took over the business on his father's retirement. Not only was William a clockmaker of distinction but he was also an inventor and amongst other things produced an instrument for automatically recording variations in mine ventilation systems, wind recorders and bells operated by steam and compressed air for use in harbour and lighthouse situations.

Here follows an advertisement for 'The Prize Medal Bailey Turret Clocks', like the one in Beckley Church, which appeared in the Silversmith's Trade Journal dated the 5th July 1875. *"In consequence of employing Steam Power and Improved Machinery PRICES ARE VERY MUCH REDUCED and have the merit of being exceedingly simple, very strong, well made, and replete with all the most modern improvements, and in consequence of being made in quantities by improved machinery, a Church Clock can be produced for less than £75 complete, which formerly could not, and cannot even now from some makers be had for more than double the price."*
There then follows various Testimonials from owners of these Turret clocks and I quote one as follows :-*"I have great pleasure in stating that I have seen Clocks made by Mr BAILEY which for WORKMANSHIP AND FINISH I think superior to ANY I HAVE SEEN BY OTHER MAKERS. I consider Mr BAILEYS charges very moderate."*
Richard Roberts.

Further Testimonials received from the Right Hon. the
Earl of Rosse F.R.S.; Chancellor of Dublin University; the
Right Rev, the Lord Bishop of Manchester, and other
distinguished learned personages, sufficiently demonstrate
the superiority of the Public Clocks erected by Bailey & Co.
They perform equally well in Northern Russia or Finland, in
Jamaica or South America as in this country.   The capital
letters in the above are copied exactly as in the Victorian text.

William was educated at Manchester Grammar School
and was an original promoter for the building of the
Manchester Ship Canal and in 1886 became one of its
directors, subscribing largely to its capital. He entered the
Salford Town Council in 1874 and was made an alderman in
1880 and mayor in 1893. In May 1894, while he was Mayor of
Salford, Queen Victoria visited Salford for the purpose of
opening the new Ship Canal and on this the first occasion of a
ship sailing through, she knighted our Beckley clockmaker.

Apart from his activities at the Albion Works and on the
Salford Council, Sir William found time to devote to
numerous other occupations and interests, some of which
follow here:-

He delivered a large number of addresses and lectures
on engineering, scientific, literary, educational and social
subjects. Sir William was most widely read in English
Literature. He was President of the Library Association of the
United Kingdom in 1906 and had been president of many
societies including the Manchester Shakespeare Society, the
Manchester Literary and Philosophical Society and the
Manchester Dickens Fellowship.

The world of the eminent maker of Beckley Church Clock seems far removed from the Parish Church but it is thanks to him and to those who wind the clock regularly that we are still able to see and hear the hour, as Beckley residents have done for well over a hundred years.

Simon C.Hogg. 1998.
From details kindly provided by Mike Bundock. Herne Bay.

Chapter Six

Beckley Characters

The Village Baker   Arthur Williams

Arthur Williams was a baker par excellence. He came to Beckley in 1937, taking over the bakehouse from Mr Bill Gatz whose family had run the business for many years.

The bakehouse was not very large, with its brick lined oven heated by a coal fire. The fire was situated in a short tunnel at the side of the oven, with the coal stored in the corner of the bakehouse and sacks of flour stacked around the walls. An old towel attached to a broom handle and kept in a bucket of water was used to remove cinders and ash from the floor of the oven before the tins and trays of dough were put in to bake. Metal lined wooden proving bins were used to mix the dough and when it was risen it was cut, weighed and kneaded all by hand. A concession to modernity was made later when an electric mixer was added.

The time tested methods and conditions under which the bread was prepared and baked would undoubtedly give today's health inspectors apoplectic fits, but certainly none of the modern, clinically clean, steam processed products could in any way compare with the crusty, nutty, flavoursome loaves that emanated from the Church Street bakehouse. Production was not confined to bread however. Dough cakes, fruit cakes, doughnuts, jam puffs et al, together with iced cakes of the very highest standard. At Harvest Festival time his decorative loaves shaped to look like sheaves of corn , displayed an artistic talent far beyond that normally expected of a village baker.

When the Second World War broke out, shortages of sugar, fats and fruit meant that cakes were only baked on very rare occasions. As more people joined the forces Arthur took on more rounds which eventually covered the 'Seven Otmoor Towns' and other nearby villages as well. A petrol ration was available for bread delivery but problems arose when vehicle spares became scarce and Arthur spent hours on repairs to keep on the road. It was quite usual when calling for bread to find a Morris or Ford gearbox, clutch or some other part in pieces on the bakehouse floor. Petrol power was at one time augmented by genuine horsepower in the form of a highly spirited animal with a will of his own and a nice four wheeled

Arthur Williams at the oven.

delivery cart.

I recall an occasion when helping to deliver bread along under Stowood with Arthur's sister Florrie. After leaving Lodge Farm Cottages the horse decided it was time to stretch his legs and took off at a gallop. We went past Royal Oak Farm, New Inn Farm and the White House going like the wind, with not a chance of stopping to deliver the bread, Florrie and I hanging on for grim death! By the time we reached Stanton crossroads the horse, whose name I cannot recall, was tiring and when we got to The George (now The Talkhouse) we managed to pull up, shaken, breathless and with the bread all over the back of the cart, but otherwise with only our pride injured. I still think that Arthur had bought a retired racehorse or at least a thoroughbred of some sort who was not at all happy at having to pull a bread delivery cart! We were very lucky there was not the traffic on the road in 1942 that there is today.

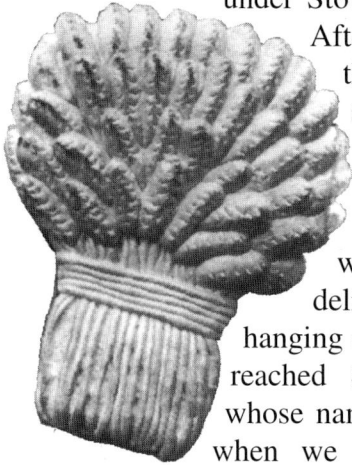

As the war progressed Arthur became busier, baking, delivering the bread and keeping his vehicle on the road. Time went haywire and he was nicknamed "The Midnight Baker" for his late hour deliveries. Neighbours often wondered when, if ever he slept. We in Church Street always knew however, when to collect our bread , the street was filled with the delicious smell of freshly baked loaves as they were removed from the oven.

Following the end of the war food shortages gradually

Loading the van outside the bakehouse

eased and Arthur returned to cake making much appreciated by ever demanding customers. But time was still in short supply and it was not unusual for him to be icing a wedding cake whilst the Bride and Groom were in the church. On one such occasion, he took the cake he had just finished up to the reception at the school, then, due to the icing still being soft, the cakes top layer started to slide off, fortunately it was caught as it was about to drop into an adjacent bowl of beetroot! The following years brought further pressures in the form of increased hygiene regulations, fierce competition from the big bakeries and burgeoning supermarkets. Arthur finally gave up the bakehouse and moved into one of the Roman Way bungalows. He then embarked on a new career, working at the crematorium, he also kept the churchyard mowed and trimmed, until shortly before his death in 1987.

And so came the end of an era. No longer were lovely freshly baked loaves and cakes available in the village and another local master craftsman had gone. The bakehouse was converted into additional living accommodation with the front door where the old oven used to be. Only the name now remains to remind us of the many palate pleasing delights we used to enjoy. But wait - when passing the Old Bakehouse as daylight fades, is it imagination - or is that the wonderful smell of newly baked bread ? Perhaps Arthur Williams ghost is still trying to catch up with that elusive time.

The Gravedigger   James Edward Shipley

For many years Jim Shipley delivered newspapers in the village and dug the graves in Beckley churchyard. He had a macabre sense of humour and on one occasion his digging was continually hindered by a local woman who wanted to gossip. The digging produced a human skull in which he placed a candle and set it up upon the heap of spoil. When the woman returned and saw the skull she made a hasty retreat leaving Jim alone to his task. The finding of bones has for a long time been a common occurrence in our churchyard and Jim used this trick on many occasions, particularly to frighten the children who used the churchyard on their way to and from school. On another occasion whilst he was finishing off digging a grave, a woman living nearby said how she disliked hearing the church bell tolling for the interment. Jim's reply was " Well my dear I shouldn't worry, as long as you can still hear it you'll know its not ringing for you!"

Hector Wheeler occasionally helped Jim particularly with some of the more difficult graves. At one time a very worried Jim rushed down to father saying "Please give me a hand, the grave has fallen in" this was at twenty to three in the afternoon and the funeral was at three ! They ran up to the churchyard carrying an old wooden door and other pieces of timber, shored up the collapsed side and dug out the soil, finishing just as the funeral procession came out of church. They then hurriedly hid behind a nearby bush until the committal was over with Jim muttering "Thank God, Thank God " over and over again.

One day Jim asked father to come and see the grave of a man who had died twelve years before, he was now opening the double grave for the burial of the mans widow who had just died. When they reached the open grave father saw a coffin at the bottom. Jim climbed down, lifted the lid and inside was a perfect skeleton. Jim took hold of the skeletons hand, shook it and said " Hello George, I didn't think I would ever see you again after all these years".

Another excavation resulted in the finding of several skeletons laid side by side, but with one with the head at the others feet. The thoughts at the time were that it was a military burial possibly from the time of the Civil War, and that the body placed the opposite way to the others was an officer or NCO. There was no indication if the remains were from the Royalist or the Parliamentarian forces. Uniforms and other military accoutrements were in such short supply at that time, that corpses were buried in just a winding sheet, so not even the clue of a belt buckle remained. In the Civil War much skirmishing took place between Wheatley and Islip on the old coaching road from London and Worcester, (now the B4027). It seems reasonable therefore to assume that these poor souls died, either as a result of such a skirmish with the enemy, or from one of the deadly diseases such as Bubonic plague or

Typhus, both of which were prevalent in the opposing armies at the time.

Jim Shipley lived in the cottage opposite the Abingdon Arms that now carries his name, although I think he may not recognise it now in its present modernised and extended form. Jim died in March 1949 at the age of 74 years and was laid to rest in the churchyard where he had laboured so often for his fellow parishioners.

The Organist   Gladys Page

Gladys Page lived with her parents at 'The Rosary' High Street, opposite the village pond. Among a wide variety of animals kept on the smallholding, was a pony which when harnessed to a two wheeled trap, was used as transport to and from Oxford. Unfortunately the pony was not very keen on pulling a loaded trap all the way to town and back, and would invariably stop and refuse to move any further than the Common Road. Gladys would then proceed to call the stubborn animal a wide range of names, none of which were to be found in the dictionaries of the time. The village lads always on the look out for a game, would watch for the trap coming then following behind waited for the fun to start. They would then add their own comments which resulted in an even fiercer tirade from Gladys, now directed at the boys as well as the pony. The proceedings usually ended with Gladys, still loudly grumbling and swearing, leading the now briskly moving pony back to its stable.

Gladys played the church organ expertly, if sometimes erratically, for many years. She would usually arrive late for the start of the service and the congregation would hear her coming several seconds before the door burst open. She wore either woolly or old trilby type hats, pulled well down on her head, a mud encrusted tweed skirt and jacket, steel tipped hobnailed boots and wrinkled stockings. She was often followed by a distinctive farmyard aroma, brought about no doubt, by having come straight from mucking out the stable! The boots would strike sparks as she clumped down the church steps and strode noisily across to the organ.

In the days before electricity came to the village and for some time after until the church could afford an electric pump, the air supply for the organ was provided by a hand pump, the prime mover generally being one of the younger members of the congregation. I can personally vouch for the fact that it was hard work! A leaded weight on a string called a 'mouse', moved up and down as an indication of the amount of air in the organ, the object being if possible, to keep the 'mouse' in the top position at all times.

When Gladys finally settled at the keyboard, she would rap loudly with her knuckles on the side of the organ to tell the blower to pump up. She would also knock loudly when, during the longer pieces of music, the blower, with arms tiring and chest heaving, tended to slow down. Her irascible nature was often apparent in her playing by using very vigorous and often violent movements of the stops, keys and pedals. During such times the congregation would often forget their singing and watch in fascination the antics on the organ, much to the annoyance of the vicar! It is true to say that Gladys' hot tempered personality dominated most services, but her boisterous playing style apart, she was always very reverent in church, with never a suggestion of the use of the rich and colourful vocabulary of which her animals heard so much.

After the death of her father in 1940 and her mother in 1941, Gladys struggled to maintain the smallholding, her organ playing suffered, and she was replaced as permanent organist, only being called upon in an emergency. In the 1950's Gladys left Beckley, to live I understand , near Banbury, so severing her links with the village.

The Airman

Jack Sidley

Strictly speaking Jack Sidley could not be called a true villager being only a temporary resident of Beckley during the Second World War, although he became by virtue of his musical talents and subsequent involvement with the village, a Beckley character. A native of Crawshawbooth in Lancashire, he came to Beckley in 1942 as a member of the Royal Air Force to serve on the Otmoor Bombing Range.

He was a very quiet man wrapped up in his love of music, an excellent piano player and in consequence very popular with his fellow service men. He preferred to play classical music but would always play popular pieces when asked. He had an uncanny and rare talent of being able to play tunes from memory just by hearing it once or looking through the sheet music. Jack would love to go anywhere where there was a piano to play, and village residents who owned one were in for a treat when he asked to come to try it out.

Having played the organ in the Methodist Chapel at his home town in Lancashire, it was a foregone conclusion that he would play in Beckley Chapel. Although it is not clear if he ever played for services in the church, he was at one time playing on the church organ a spirited rendering of "Roll out the Barrel" when he was surprised by the vicar Canon Swainson. Probably today it would be accepted in a lighter spirit, but at that time the vicar was very annoyed and severely admonished Jack for showing a lack of reverence in church.

He married a Beckley girl Gwen Hayden one of a family of five sisters living in Church Street, three of whom married men from Beckley RAF. Jack and Gwen went to live in Lancashire and some years later Jack died following an industrial accident.

Whilst stationed on Otmoor he would go for long walks and the lonely beauty of the area inspired him to write a poem about it which he later set to music.

These Lovely Things

These lovely things in life are ours to share,
Simple little things beyond compare,
The rainbow and the roses
The songbirds all day long
Dear Father thou hast made our lives a song.

These choicest gifts of thine are ours alone,
Give to us the grace to be thine own,
This beauty that enfolds us
Is wonderful and fair
These lovely things beyond compare.

These lovely things in life are ours to share,
Simple little things beyond compare,
The moonbeams and the snowdrops
The pastures wet with dew
They teach us how to live our lives anew.

When we are sad and when we kneel in prayer,
Make us just to feel that thou art there,
This beauty that enfolds us
Is wonderful and fair
These lovely things beyond compare.

Jack Sidley. Stationed at RAF Otmoor, Beckley. 1942.
The poem and information for the article kindly provided by Mary Longthorne.

The Churchwarden   Kathleen Marguerite Lea

Kate, as everyone called her, was a truly remarkable woman.

In the 1960's in anticipation of her retirement from a brilliant academic career, she bought numbers 2&3 Church Street intending eventually to move in to one of them. This she did, settling in to number 2 in 1971. Here she established a home with her books and her cats, single handedly tending the large garden. She became a member of the Parochial Church Council and in 1972 was appointed Churchwarden, a post she held until shortly before her death in 1995.

Kate was seemingly indefatigable, although suffering from failing eyesight and asthma, one never heard a word of complaint. She was to be found weeding the church paths, tending the flowers, helping at the school and Sunday school, showing visitors around the church, as well as entertaining her many friends, neighbours, former colleagues and pupils to meals in her cottage. She also always rang the church bell for Sunday services and locked and unlocked the church night and morning.

I recall being out walking with Phyllis and our dog Tosh, one bitter winter day with snow being blown

94

horizontally by a vicious east wind. Along the Common Road we met Kate delivering church leaflets. Although obviously having trouble with her breathing, she greeted us with a cheerful grin and saying " We should all be indoors on a day like this, but there - Tosh is enjoying it." On another occasion we were driving home on the road from Elsfield when we came across Kate sat in her car with her chin on her chest, fearing she was unwell, we stopped and in answer to our question, "Was she alright?" She lifted her head, smiled broadly and said "Thank you so much, I was just resting my eyes". I was passing her cottage one day and she came to the door laughing and chuckling and said "I have been listening to what I thought was a cricket chirping in my hearth, but I've just found out it is the smoke detector battery that needs replacing".

The care and affection shown to her cats was reciprocated by the companionship they gave, whilst the names she gave them reflected her sense of humour and fun. There was Oliver, who like his Dickens namesake was forever asking for more. Will o' the Wisp, Willow for short because he was here, there and everywhere, travelling fast and seldom touching down. Then there was Worcester, so called because he was so full of sauce! Worcester was particularly fond of Kate's home made cakes and was not averse to stealing pieces from visitors plates.

Kathleen Marguerite Lea was born in Chorley, Lancashire and was educated at Wycombe Abbey School. In 1921 she won a scholarship to Lady Margaret Hall in Oxford and after taking a first in English returned to Wycombe Abbey to teach. She was awarded a Suzette Taylor Research Travelling Fellowship which enabled her to spend two years in Italy studying Italian Renaissance poetry and painting, and the Commedia del Arte on which she based her first published book, Italian Popular Comedy (1934). From 1926 to 1937 she was a lecturer at Westfield College and then returned to Lady Margaret Hall as Tutor and Fellow. From 1947 until her retirement in 1971 she held the position of Vice-Principle.

Kate will be remembered by all who knew her not only for her academic brilliance and prodigious memory, but also her courtesy, kindness, wit, wisdom, a marvellous sense of humour and her dogged independence. A former pupil, having produced some indifferent work said "Her honesty would not let either her or me ignore a thoroughly unsatisfactory piece of work. Her kindness on the other hand, made her shrink from causing pain however well deserved."

The Lea Library by Vanessa Ross

I have just started at Headington Girls School which is very big and has two libraries: the main one is for older girls and the Lea Library is for juniors. It is named after Miss Kate Lea who lived near us in Church Street, Beckley. Miss Lea, a Don at Oxford University had been a governor of Headington School and Vice-Principal of Lady Margaret Hall for many years. I remember her going to the church every day to unlock and clean, and garden in the churchyard. Headington School Library was dedicated to her after she died in 1995.

Written by Vanessa in 1998

The Horseman   George Thomas Newell

George Newell was born at Lower Woods Farm, a true man of Otmoor with an enduring interest in horses that persisted from boyhood throughout his life. The family later moved to Bee Cottage in Church Street Beckley a lovely old cottage overlooking the church.

During the first World War George served in the Queen's Own (Oxfordshire) Hussars which was a crack horse Regiment, and for most of the war was in action in France and Belgium. During the battles around Ypres he had a particularly dreadful time where three horses were shot from beneath him but fortunately he went through the war and returned home unscathed. Back in civilian life he became a trainer of horses and was employed by some of the best studs. One well known owner once said "He is the best judge of horse flesh in the country". He also taught one of the foreign Crown Princes to ride.

A very good looking man, tall with blue eyes always particularly well groomed and generously gifted with much charm, which he knew how to use most skilfully. He hunted with the Bicester Hounds who were "A bit of a rough bunch - not so upmarket as the Heythrop". He rode frequently with Major Miller of Shotover House, and by all accounts they were a couple of tear-aways, enjoyed every minute of one another's company, especially after a large gin or two. On one occasion he requested a testimonial which was gladly given, and in the words of the referee - "He fears neither God nor the Devil" which speaks for itself.

George's mother was a shrewd capable country woman

very much thought of in Beckley especially at the 'big house' - The Grove. Her home-made parsnip and other wines were famous and were the talk and envy of the village and around the area. When her son had been married a year she said to his pretty young wife - "Well my girl, now that you have wintered him and summered him what do you think of him? - I couldn't do anything with him!" His wife then once said, "He would sit up all night with a sick horse, but wouldn't sit up with me !" Among other things he was fearless. On one occasion a rough band of gypsies had camped on his land and troubled his wife by their persistent begging. He confronted them one morning in the early hours carrying just a lantern and demanded they leave as soon as it grew light or suffer the consequences. They left within the hour.

He attempted to teach my sister and I to ride. I was far too nervous to make any headway but my sister mastered it quickly to his complete satisfaction and amusement. She found this of particular use in later years when in the Women's Land Army. This character was in fact my father, I miss him to this day, particularly some of his sayings, - such as "A lean dog for a hard road" and "Follow a straight road and you won't get lost." I have always tried to be guided by this last piece of advice and have reached my goals whilst others have changed direction so many times and failed in their endeavours.

My father was particularly loyal to his own family, had an infectious sense of humour and sparkle. At almost ninety years of age he was like a stick of dynamite. His wish was that his ashes be scattered "Where the fox runs over the spinney between Horton and Noke Wood"(Horton Spinney).

(From an article by Mrs E.K.Parnell written in 1997).

Beckley Reflects

The Poet *(among other things)*   Richard (Dickie) Coles

Dickie Coles was a bachelor who lived in Otmoor Lane. Apparently he was very fond of animals and kept a large number of cats, never knowing quite how many because when he sharpened his knife to prepare their food, cats from all around also came for a meal! (The area still has many cats today!) He was a great prankster and would amuse the village children with all manner of tricks, one in particular involved him appearing to swallow a frog, some were convinced that he did indeed swallow it, others maintained he hid it in his magnificent white beard. Unfortunately there is not much more information available about him, and this is an example of not finding things out before the people that knew him passed away. He died in 1923 at the age of 85 years. The following poem written by Dickie was originally published in the Beckley Parish Magazine in 1876.

Beckley

A pleasant place, place of delight
In ancient times renowned,
'Ere Oxford towers or Woodstock bowers
A place or name had found.
A prospect wide up Chilterns side
Nearby the east doth lie,
And northward-ho on the moor below
The Ray streams sluggish by.
A mighty prince that's long dead since
Did favour our sweet town,
He built a tower the Danes to cower
This tower now pulled down.
The Romans too, conquest in view

99

A camp and dwelling had,
Their coins are found upon the ground
Their urns down in the Slad.
And here doth rest the body blest
Of St Donaver, they say, they say,
A Saxon true, now lost to view
By saints of later day.
'Tis worth your while in Mary's aisle
Blest Mary there to see,
With her sweet child, the undefiled
Sweet Jesus on her knee.
Of purest springs and other things
Which to us all belong,
I'll not refuse, if you so choose
To write another song.

John and Ann Wing have an original manuscript in Dickie's very spidery writing which tends one to the belief that the three poems therein were written late in his life. Two of them are below and a further poem about the Otmoor riots is reproduced in chapter four.

I went for a walk one day

I met a man, and asked him why
They had a service there but once a week
He said Parson did not think it right
To act so much like Puseyite.
I found a padlock on the door
No service there for rich or poor
Oh wretched scene, oh horrid sight
But no one called it Puseyite.
In prison too it cant be right
With bars put up to stop the light

This surely is not Puseyite.
At Xmas you should fill them tight
At New Year, their friends invite
Then let them have a pipe to light
Oh no you say, that wont do quite
They and every one turn Puseyite.

The Puseyites were a religious movement started by an Anglican cleric Edward Pusey (1800 -1882) in Oxford in 1833. He published Tracts for the Times which inaugurated the Tractarian movement that developed into what became known as Puseyism. The object of the movement was to show that Protestantism could be made to square with Roman Catholic doctrine. The increasing tendency however towards Roman liturgy and ceremonials was widely resented. Another of the founder leaders John Henry Newman changed over to Roman Catholicism in 1845.

The Ranters Ship

The Ranters ship is now set sail
Sometimes we have a pleasing gale
But sometimes the sea is rough
But Jesus speaks and that's enough
Come all you wretched slaves of sin
Your captain now will take you in
Sing Glory Alleluia.
Come drunkards, sinners, swearers too
Come and join the favoured few
For when you are born again
You'll do.
Sing Glory Alleluia.

The Ranters was a derisive term applied to early vigorous Methodist preaching.

'Dickie' Coles and his cats in a very old photograph.

Chapter Seven

Progress ?

Three Lights and a Plug

Our village started to catch up with the 20th century when, just before the Second World War the Wessex Electricity Company, prompted by a request from the Royal Air Force for an electricity supply to the bombing range on Otmoor, decided to provide it in Beckley as well. I n a comparatively short time the villagers were canvassed to see how many would be interested in taking a supply, there must have been enough to make it a viable proposition because routes were then surveyed, wayleaves negotiated, poles erected, cables strung, houses wired and meters fitted. The village was fed by an 11kv transformer mounted on a wooden pole at the bottom of Sandy Path. From there the low voltage overhead supply cables ran on roughly the same routes as today.

In order to encourage the use of electricity the Wessex Company offered to install free of charge, three lights and one plug socket. Many villagers took up the offer, the more affluent households adding extra circuits. House wiring in those days was rubber insulated and lead sheathed and installed with extreme care so as not to kink or crease the lead sheath, which resulted in damage to the rubber insulation and copper conductors beneath. The impact on the village of the installations was to say the least 'electric', no longer was it necessary to fill and trim smelly paraffin lamps, or go to bed with candles, and even with just 'three and a plug' life was indeed transformed. Many villages had to wait until after the war to get electricity and thanks must go to the RAF who wanted a supply. We in Beckley might not have got it until

The street lamp at Church Corner, installed in 1897 to celebrate Queen Victoria's diamond jubilee

after the war if the bombing range had not been there.

The domestic appliances available at the time were of quite basic design and relatively expensive compared with today. In consequence apart from the lights, most houses had just an electric kettle, later adding a small cooker and perhaps a wash boiler to replace the old solid fuel or paraffin oil cooking ranges and coppers. The exciting prospect of more labour saving appliances was unfortunately postponed by the outbreak of war in 1939, when development and production of anything other than essential items ceased in deference to the war effort. It was not until the 1950's when cookers, refrigerators, washing machines, and television sets became more widely available and within the financial reach of more people. Even then the appliances were not nearly so sophisticated as those of today.

When the Queen's Coronation took place in 1953 there were not many television sets in the village. Friends and neighbours gathered in the houses that had sets to watch the processions and the ceremony in Westminster Abbey. Most of the sets had tiny 9 inch screens and fortunate indeed were those who possessed a 12 inch model. Beckley Mast had not been erected at that time and transmissions came from Sutton Coldfield, this meant that large unsightly outside aerials were needed, thankfully no longer necessary, although now of course we have satellite dishes. So much for progress !

The demand for electricity grew over the years, extra transformers and re-enforcement's were needed to supplement the network. By this time the Wessex Electricity Company had long since ceased to exist, nationalisation in 1948 having formed the Southern Electricity Board as the responsible authority for supply and distribution of electricity in our area. More recently the industry has been returned to the private sector, as a result of mergers the company is now Scottish and Southern Energy plc, and now they can sell gas as well! And we can buy our energy anywhere else. All very confusing to one used to the old days.

The first electric street lamp was installed at the Church corner during bitter winter weather in February 1947. The Wessex Electricity Company quotation for the work was £12 with an annual charge for electricity and maintenance of £2 7s

6d (£2.37 ½) I remember the job well as it was one of the first I did on my return to 'civvy street,' and after being used to the heat of the Far East, I felt at the time that Church Corner must have been one of the coldest places on earth! This was not the first lamp at this site however, old photographs show an iron column on the corner of High Street with Church Street opposite the church gate. The lamp was erected by the Parish in 1897 to celebrate Queen Victoria's Diamond Jubilee. The installation was carried out by Messrs Wyatt and Son of Oxford for the sum of £3 10s 3d (£3.51). Illumination was by means of an oil lamp. Members of old Beckley families namely H.Wing, Charles Newell, Martin Newell, and E.Hudson, attended to the lamp during its working years, filling with oil, trimming the wick and presumably manually turning it on and off night and morning. The annual running cost was initially £2 which was increased to £2 5s (£2.25) in 1901. These costs are almost as much as those initially charged for the electric lamp installed 50 years later. The lamp was taken out of commission in 1915 because of the threat of air raids by German Zeppelins although I don't think they ever penetrated as far as Beckley. The Parish Council at a meeting in 1932 discussed re-lighting the lamp, but no action was taken other than suggesting that it could perhaps be financed by private subscription, an option that was never taken up, so the lamp must have gradually fallen into disrepair. I remember the column being there but with no lantern on top. There were never any signs at that time that the lamp was painted, the metal always being rusty. In 1950 Henry Wakelin who owned the property adjoining the lamp, was given permission to remove it providing that he repaid to the Parish Council any money he received for the scrap value! No mention was made of the outcome, although the column was removed about this time.

And so the future for electricity in our village? It is certain that we shall continue to need it in increasing quantities, but might we dare hope that the financial curbs that inhibit the placing of overhead cables underground be somehow overcome? Although several efforts have been made over the years to get something done, what has been achieved has been mainly cosmetic and affecting only a few properties. A similar exercise in Stanton-St-John a few years ago did I understand, cost the parishioners quite a lot of money, and the Electricity Companies are not inclined to spend their profits on such projects. Perhaps some system of power distribution will in future be devised whereby no poles or cables are required ? No longer need we fear a loss of supply during gales or thunderstorms, and our village would be so much better without the poles and cables.

"It's Good to talk"

The 17th century writer of the rhyme in which the people of Beckley 'spoke directly,' would no doubt have endorsed the onetime slogan used by British Telecom "Its good to talk" as very relevant to our village. Had telephones been in existence then, Beckley parishioners would probably have been very good customers.

It was not until 1925 that the GPO (General Post Office)

at that time responsible for the telephone system as well as the mail, brought the telephone to Beckley. Before then a telegraph to the old Post Office in Church Street provided a link to the outside world. It is not known when this system came in to operation, but old photographs taken around the turn of the century show poles and wires in position at that time.

At 11.30am on 30th of December 1925, nine telephone subscribers were connected from a manually operated exchange situated in Stanton St. John Post Office, covering

---

Times of Availability
Week days 8.00am to 8.00pm.
Sundays   9.00am to 10.30am. and 4.00pm to 6.00pm.
The numbers connected were:-
No 1   Telephone Kiosk, Stanton-St-John.
No 2   The Hon W.W.Holland-Hibbert, Grove House Beckley.
No 3   Mr Henderson, Studley Priory.
No 4   Mr Guy Thompson, Woodperry House.
No 5   Telephone Kiosk, Elsfield.
No 6   Mr Weatherby, Stanton House.
No 7   Mr John Buchan, Elsfield Manor.
No 8   Mr Loxley, Bayswater Road.
No 9   Mr Fielding, Beckley Park.

---

the villages of Stanton, Beckley, Elsfield and Horton-cum-Studley.

Six subscribers, Nos. 2,3,4,6,7and 9, were given night service by means of through switching to the Oxford Exchange. Strangely, Beckley villagers did not have access to a public telephone at this time, perhaps the GPO had never heard of the old rhyme ?

Not many more subscribers were connected before the end of the decade, but two of note were No 11, the Abingdon Arms and No 12, Beckley Post Office. At that time Beckley did not have a kiosk, but villagers could use the telephone in the Post Office. The Office was first situated in Church Street in the house now known as Newridge, then afterwards in the new shop built at Stoneycroft, High Street. Mr Amos Wing the Sub-Postmaster would take messages and being the Telegraph Officer delivered telegrams in the village and also to Noke and Elsfield. The deliveries which were carried out night and day and in all weathers, resulted in some awful journeys over the years.

On 28th February 1933 the exchange was transferred to new premises in Stanton and then on 9th February 1957, the old manual board was replaced by an automatic system. This meant that Mr Frank Knight the Sub-Postmaster and Miss F. Barrett, the telephone operator (Bessie to all the subscribers,) became, as far as the telephone system was concerned, redundant - the 'personal touch' was gone forever from the telephone system in this area.

Modern electronic equipment replaced the old electro-mechanical exchange on 12th December 1992 giving much clearer lines, faster dialling and enabling many innovative uses of the telephone to be brought into use. The old Stanton St.John Exchange numbers were replaced by the prefix 35 or 351, and using the Oxford Exchange dialling code. Meanwhile, apart from the technological improvements, administrative changes were also taking place. In 1981 the postal and telephone services split to form the Post Office, (responsible for the mail) and Post Office Telecommunications (for the telephone system.) In 1984 the

The growth of telephones in our area on the Stanton Exchange			
Date	Lines connected	Date	Lines connected
1925	9	1936	39
1926	11	1937	41
1927	12	1938	44
1928	13	1939	43
1929	15	1946	55
1930	17	1951	60
1931	17	1953	79
1932	17	1963	188
1933	23	1973	439
1934	28	1983	542
1935	31	1993	790
No records are available for the years not noted.			

telecommunications were privatised forming British Telecom.

So to the future, it holds out exciting prospects of many new services becoming available from our telephone lines. There are already many options in information technology for business and leisure facilities, being brought directly into our homes, with rapid technological advances making the possibilities seemingly endless. I have reservations however on the use of Video-Phones; "It's good to talk"- but perhaps not so good to see and be seen? Or perhaps:-

No need to go to Beckley
To be seen directly
(With apologies to our 17th century writer.)

Sweet Water and Smelly Waste

Mains water was brought to the village in 1947, thereby bringing to an end the years of dependence on the many wells and springs. Some houses had their own well and there were several communal ones around the village. The occupants of houses with wells spent a lot of time pumping and those without wells carrying the buckets of water home. When Midsummer Cottage in Church Street was bombed and set on fire in 1943, it was due to the time it took to pump and fill buckets and carry them from the wells, that caused the fire to get so firm a hold. It was fortunate that no other buildings were hit as there was not the means to contain a bigger outbreak. The existing well in Church Street is not very deep but the water used to be clear and sweet. Problems always followed a thunder storm when the street drains would become blocked with leaves, stones and gravel the result was that the dirty storm water would run into the well. After the storm the first task was to bucket the dirty water out of the well, and wait for the spring to fill it up with clear water which would usually take about four hours. The drains still block today of course, although the blockage in addition to the leaves etc, is now more likely to be aggravated by discarded take away food cartons, crisp packets or sweet wrappings - there's progress for you!

When finally there was a supply of water on tap, the villagers thoughts turned to removing another cause of drudgery by installing indoor water closets, and so doing away with the insanitary methods of sewage disposal that had been in use for centuries. In the past lavatories were invariably situated, for obvious reasons, at the end of the garden, not exactly the nicest place to visit on a dark windy night or on a cold frosty morning! Some dwellings had large pits that needed to be dug out every few years, others had a big bucket that had to be emptied at least once a week or else you had an unpleasant smelly overflow. It was usual for the spoil from both types to be dug into gardens or spread on to fields, which would produce extremely fine flower and vegetable crops, and is probably responsible for many of the fertile gardens that we have in our village today. I must just mention the multi-hole seats that existed in many of the old lavatories, apparently the whole family would visit together, could this be yet another version of the saying that 'the family that '-----' together stays together' ? Perhaps someone could suggest that multi-seated loos might contribute to reducing today's high divorce rate? What a thought! I know of one such seat in Beckley that has been preserved, but not of course still in use, the building is now a useful garden store.

In the early 1970's a sewage disposal system was proposed for the village by the then Local Authority, Bullingdon Rural District Council. The scheme was planned, surveyed and pipe runs actually pegged. Everyone was pleased that the septic tanks and cess pits would soon be things of the past, septic tanks although an improvement on the older cesspits still accrued problems with their soak-aways. Alas it was not meant to be. In 1974, it was decided that local government was in need of re-organisation. The Bullingdon RDC became the South Oxfordshire District Council and much more importantly the main responsibility for sewage disposal was transferred from the District Councils to the newly formed Water Boards. Thames Water is an organisation covering a big area of which our village is a very small part. In consequence the Beckley sewerage scheme was shelved, and has assumed a very low priority with the installation costs escalating dramatically over the years. We now seem to have very little hope of anything happening in either the near or distant future.

It is somewhat ironic that with all the technology available today, we can put men on the moon, and communicate by sound and vision in seconds with anywhere in the world, yet here we are welcoming in a new millennium, one of only a few villages in the country without the means to collectively dispose of our effluent cleanly and efficiently.

Up To His Neck In It
A true story of what can happen if you try to save money.

Until the post war years the school toilets were situated near where the pool pumps are today. The waste dropped into a big cesspit alongside the toilets and the pit was concealed by a large wooden cover. When the pit was full the contents were dug out by hand and spread on gardens, allotments or fields. This was a dirty and for the neighbours a very malodorous method of sewage disposal, but as there was then no other alternative, common in the village at that time.

In the late 1920's a school managers meeting was held on site to discuss the suspected deterioration of the wooden cover, and the meeting was attended by my father to give any practical advice required. The then incumbent, the Revd. Kinchin-Smith, thought that the cover would last a few more years, and to prove his point, and despite warnings from others present, he proceeded to do a dance on it. Suddenly the whole thing collapsed and the vicar disappeared down into the mire. He was dragged out fortunately unhurt, but in a filthy state and the meeting was swiftly abandoned.

Soon after my father made and fitted a new cover which lasted until the pit was eventually filled in when mains water came to the village in 1947, and when flush toilets and a septic tank were installed.

Gas

Bottled only, no draught available!

Chapter Eight

Win Some Lose Some

From the Enclosure Acts
to the present day

Our predecessors in the early Nineteenth Century certainly had a fight on their hands against the Enclosure Acts for Otmoor, and lost the battle with results that must have been disastrous for many families. Although not threatening to our livelihood or degenerating into violence, there have been several times over recent years when our area has been threatened by developments that had they gone ahead would have severely affected many aspects of our village life. Probably the most alarming was when routes for the M40 extension were proposed across Otmoor, on various alignments and including some practically on the doorsteps of Lower Farm and the 16th century Beckley Park. This particular threat hung over us for many years through the interminable process of consultation and enquiry. It was always a source of amazement to me that, having been told by local inhabitants that the Otmoor area was prone to sudden and thick fogs, highway engineers could even think of building a road in such a place. Apparently the series of fog tests that were carried out near Lower Farm were held during some of the driest months for years, and in consequence gave a quite distorted result. Often in the mornings even in early summer, we in Beckley can be enjoying clear sunshine whilst the moor is heavily shrouded in mist with only the tops of the tallest trees showing, a phenomenon that could have spelt disaster on a motorway in that position.

A battle lost was the one to retain the village Post Office. After the closure of the long serving shop run for many years by successive generations of the Wing family, efforts to establish a Post Office and stores in other premises only lasted until 1974, when Beckley's pensioners were told to collect their dues from Stanton St John (the nearest) or any other Post Office of their choice. There were then about 75 pensioners out of a population of around 400, so the MP for Mid-Oxon, Mr Douglas Hurd was contacted and as a result he had protracted discussions and correspondence with the Post Office. Many solutions were suggested such as hiring rooms in various premises (including the pub!) on pension days and using a mobile post office, some were tried and all were eventually rejected mainly for reasons of security caused by the situation of large sums of money being present at the same place and time every week. As the problem affected many other places than just our village, Douglas Hurd raised the matter in the House of Commons. All efforts came to no avail, the problem still ongoing, is a social one brought about by the changing patterns of village life. It is widespread, has caused, and is still causing many problems in rural communities bereft of basic essential services.

Since the Television Transmitter was installed at Beckley, originally by the BBC, the progress of television broadcasting and communications technology has brought about a proliferation in the arrays of apparatus and buildings on the site, so much so that the aerial now resembles a giant Christmas tree with its seedlings and dishes like huge flowers. With continuing demand for more TV channels and telecommunications, all prompted and encouraged undoubtedly by big business interests, things are likely to get much worse. I understand there is little that can be done to limit 'progress' on the site. The present owners of the site, have as a concession offered to carry out tree planting and landscaping. One victory by the village however was over the 'Flashing Lights' issue, explained later in the article by Frank Ratford.

The proposed closure of the road through Elsfield was suggested by the residents of that village prompted by the increase in vehicular traffic speeding through. Although one sympathised with the reasons for the request, it never the less came as a shock to the residents of Beckley, as that way was always our traditional route to Oxford. This was the road the carriers used and the farmers took to market, and when Beckley had its own bus service, this was the route the buses came. For those of us that attended schools or worked in Oxford, it was the way we cycled back and forth. It does not appear that road closures can ever be a final solution, although it may solve one problem, the traffic will only be diverted through to the next village, and so on, and then - where do you stop? Fortunately through the sterling efforts of Anne Purse our County and District Councillor (who was in the unenviable position of representing both villages), and by Frank Ratford whose diligence revealed that the figures on which the decision for closure would be based were badly flawed, a compromise was reached, and the road stayed open, so preserving the long established access from Beckley through Elsfield and on to Oxford.

Disproving the figures   by Frank Ratford

Having learned of the proposal by Oxfordshire Highways Authority to put a gate at the B4027 end of the road to Elsfield, to close the road due to dangerously high traffic movements through the village, I managed to obtain a copy of the traffic figures shown on a meter that had been installed. Upon examination it became obvious that a serious error existed in the figures for traffic in the morning/afternoon peak periods, as an almost equal number was shown for traffic flow in both directions - something that was not happening. I contacted Anne Purse our local Councillor, and I arranged to conduct a traffic count during both peak periods, to be held over one week. As a result I discovered that, whilst in the mornings the traffic count towards Oxford was almost the same as the Council's figures, that in the opposite direction was less than 10% of their stated number. In the afternoons the flow away from Oxford was similar to the Council figures, but again the opposite flow was a mere trickle. This was a puzzle, so after three days I shifted my observation point so that I was close to the Flow Meter, I then found that the sensors which operate when a vehicle passed over had been placed in such a way that they were registering movement in both directions every time a car passed. Thus the figures showed a substantial increase in the actual traffic movements. The facts were duly sent to the Highways Authority and Anne Purse.

The gate was not installed, but road humps were put down. Although they are inconvenient, we still have our long established way to Oxford, even if we do 'get the hump' before we get there.

Frank Ratford 1999

It is often surprising how quickly a simple thing like new lights on a television mast can seriously affect our way of life. The consequences of the BBC's action in replacing the old red warning lights by bright white flashing ones was felt not only in Beckley but in other villages around, and resulted in a concerted action which brought about the compromise related here by Frank Ratford. Incidentally I am assured that the occupants of the houses around the aerial did not, as was reported, garden at night by the light of the 'flashers'

The Beckley Flasher   by Frank Ratford

One evening in April 1991, I was driving home along the Northern-by-pass when I became aware of brilliant flashes lighting up the northern sky. My passengers remarked on this and we became very concerned when we turned for Elsfield and saw the flashing came from the TV mast in our village. There had been no public notice of any thing happening on the mast and we assumed that an electrical fault had developed. Unfortunately it went on all night and despite having thick lined curtains it was impossible to shut out the brilliant flashes from the bedroom. The next day I contacted the BBC and the Oxford Mail to complain and was told that the old lights were worn out and that a new 'European Union Directive' required replacement with flashing lights on all masts over 600ft (Beckley's is 630ft).

The BBC engineer made the excuse that the lights should be reduced in power after dark and that this would be done in the future. However the nuisance persisted and a Parish Meeting was held to discuss the matter with the BBC, Civil Aviation Authority and other interested bodies. By this time other villages affected were joining us and a small committee was formed to handle the protest.

Various avenues were explored and then we found out from the International Air Traffic Authority that there was in fact no such 'E.U. Directive' which applied to the Beckley Mast. Faced with this fact the BBC agreed to compromise by replacing the red lights to show at all times, and the flashing lights only to be on during daylight hours, the situation as it exists today.

Frank Ratford. 1999.

And so we come to what was probably the greatest threat to Beckley, or indeed the other 'Seven Towns' since the Acts of Enclosure of Otmoor, The M40 Extension. The period of time during which schemes were submitted and enquiries carried out seemed interminable and was in fact over twenty years. The whole story of the extended battle and eventual victory, is ably set out below by Bob Bixby who was in the front line taking a prominent part in the fight to divert the motorway away from Otmoor.

The M40   by Bob Bixby

The extension of the M40 from Wheatley to Birmingham had been planned since the 1960's and various proposals had been put forward but eventually, in the early 1980's the government published it's preferred alignment. The road was to run on a two metre high embankment on the mainly low lying land from Waterstock, below Stanton Great Wood to the east of Beckley Park and then across the eastern part of Otmoor before crossing the road between Fencott and

Murcott and joining the A43 (now A34) at Wendlebury. Various groups, individuals and organisations actively campaigned against the proposals and the Parish Council aligned itself with the Otmoor Group which included a representative from each of the 'Seven Towns'. The main thrust of our case was to raise the profile of Otmoor by emphasising its physical, social, landscape and ecological qualities and the way in which the road would affect these and the delicate balance between the moor and it's 'towns'. A technical rebuttal of the government's case was also mounted as we objected strongly to their main justification for the motorway was to provide relief to the M1 between London and Birmingham. The campaign relied entirely on voluntary effort and mounting it dominated the lives of the group for the year before the enquiry and also during the 110 days of the enquiry itself.

At the end of the enquiry the Inspector recommended against the Otmoor section and the view appeared to be endorsed by the Minister in his decision letter. Because an alternative route had to be worked out and the various statutory procedures, including another public enquiry, gone through there was a real prospect of the M40 being opened from Wendlebury to Birmingham without the missing link across Otmoor. The likelihood of such a delay had already been raised at the enquiry but now the possibility that the B4027 could become the missing motorway link, carrying traffic diverted from the M1, was a real prospect. The Parish Council was very active in campaigning to avoid such a situation arising.

The second public enquiry into the missing Otmoor section of the motorway, now on a more eastern alignment, opened in 1986 and surprisingly at the opening the Inspector ruled that he felt obliged to consider routes across Otmoor as well as elsewhere. during the course of the enquiry, which lasted another 70 days, 22 routes between Wick Farm and Merton were considered nearly all of which affected Beckley or Otmoor. It was very time consuming to monitor the arguments made by their proposers and counter them all as it was not considered sensible to rely on the Department of Transport to argue strongly against Otmoor routes as, after all one of them had been their original choice! At the end of that enquiry the eastern route was confirmed although the Inspector showed considerable sympathy for a route skirting the edge of Oxford and incorporating Headington and North Oxford bypasses.

The fight to protect Otmoor from the threat of the M40 was one of the most effective campaigns there has been and, very unusually, managed to force the abandonment of the Department of Transport's preferred route even though it had the support of the local authorities. Those who committed themselves to the campaign and gave up so much of their time did so because of a strong belief that a motorway across the moor would destroy something precious. Their view is summarised in the following brief edited extract from the Otmoor Group's closing statement :

"If Otmoor is to be valued, and the evidence that Otmoor has value is we feel irrefutable, then one must ask oneself ; can Otmoor absorb this road without irreparable damage being done to it? Do not be misled by that strange feeling of remoteness which one feels as one crosses the moor as the horizon seems to slip away. Rather go up to one of the vantage points above the moor, for example the Beckley Hill, where the small scale of the moor becomes clear. Then imagine for a moment a dual lane motorway - embankment, hardshoulder, three lanes of traffic, centre reserve, another three lanes, another hardshoulder and embankment ploughing its way at just above hedge top level for eight kilometres from below Horton to Fencott, Murcott and beyond - and ask yourself : could this place be remotely as it is today if the road was to pass through it ?

(Bob Bixby. 1999.)

There have been several proposals to turn Otmoor into a giant reservoir to supply water for London and the Lower Thames valley, various schemes having been put forward from time to time since the mid 1930's. I don't suppose that visually it would have been too horrific from our village, but the plan to build a fifty to sixty foot high bank to contain the water would have probably put five of the other "Otmoor Towns" in permanent shade, as well as the total inundation of Beckley Park, Lower Farm and the surrounding areas. This scheme could well be resurrected again in the future, and what has gone before may only have been preliminary skirmishes, so fellow residents of the Otmoor 'towns' we must stay on our guard!

High Street Beckley 1905

High Street Beckley 1965

Chapter Nine

Beckley Weather

These sayings were often used in our village, and some of them are common to places other than Beckley.

It used to be said that if, in Beckley, you could clearly hear the trains leaving Islip Station for Bicester and Bletchley, it would rain before very long. That was in the days of steam trains, now sadly no longer with us. The sounds of the diesels are obviously not the same, and they are not so good at predicting the weather. Similarly, the same is said of Charlton church bells, when they are clearly heard in Beckley rain will surely follow.

When pheasants keep up a continual "Cock Up Cock Up" call, it means that thunder is on the way.

The saying is that fogs in March will mean frosts on the same dates in May.

Wherever the wind is on the 15th of April it will mainly stay there until the 15th of June.

An abundance of blackthorn blossom in May, usually means a cold spell of weather called a "Blackthorn Winter". Very often true.

Rain before seven, fine before eleven.

If the sun goes pale to bed, It will rain tomorrow, so 'tis said.

Cows and sheep lie down when fine weather is coming, (in some areas it means just the opposite, and that it will rain). All very confusing.

A ring around the moon foretells rain.

When larks fly high and sing long, expect fine weather (if you are lucky enough to find some larks these days).

Swallows flying high means the weather will be dry. Both this and the previous one about the larks is most likely true because the insects on which they feed fly higher as a fine spell approaches.

Red sky at night, shepherds delight. (fine.)

Red sky in the morning, shepherds warning. (wet and windy.)

These last two are probably some of the oldest sayings, being mentioned in the Bible :-

When it is evening, you say, It will be fair weather: for the sky is red. And in the morning, It will be stormy weather today: for the sky is red and overcast.

Matthew 16 v.2,3.

Some of the sayings can certainly be proved to be true and were the result of long observation and experience by our ancestors, but because weather patterns can change so quickly, they don't always work out. In fact some of them can turn out to be pure rubbish! But when you think about it, the weather forecasters of today, even with the use of all their modern technical aids, quite often get it wrong.

Some Bad Weather times

The following was written in the family bible belonging to Roger Payne whose family lived in our village for over one hundred and fifty years. The notes refer to a period of very severe weather in Beckley in the nineteenth century.

1849

April 17th,
 sharp frost at night.

18th & 19th sharp frost and snow in the daytime.

The 20th, very heavy storm of snow and hail and lightening and thunder in the afternoon.

In November 1927, Caleb Clarke of Stowood was buried in Beckley churchyard, after being killed by a falling tree in Elsfield during a terrific storm on the 16th of November.

Otmoor was regularly flooded every winter until it was extensively drained in the 1970's. Before then it was often possible in severe weather, to skate from any of the 'Seven Towns,' right across the moor and into Oxford by joining the frozen River Cherwell at Islip.

The two worst winters in recent memory were in 1947 and 1962/3, when on both occasions the village was 'snowed in' for a time, although some of us remember the bad one during January and February 1940. In 1947 not many in the parish owned cars and most of us managed to get to work by walking through the snowdrifts. In the aftermath of the war most things were either rationed or unobtainable, and life was quite grim enough without having to put up with the period of awful weather which went on for about five weeks, followed by severe flooding on Otmoor and other areas.

In 1962 it started to snow during the afternoon of Christmas Day, and the freeze kept on for over two months into 1963. By this time more people owned cars, but often could not get them out of the village. The roads would be cleared, then along came another blizzard and they were impassable again, it just seemed to go on and on. The road from the village past the White House down to Bayswater was cleared with just a single traffic lane through the four feet deep drifts. On a lovely sunny but cold Saturday morning in January, we ventured to Headington for supplies and as the east wind was rising and blowing the snow off the adjoining fields, we asked the butcher to serve us quickly as we were afraid the road would soon be blocked again. He could not believe it, as the only snow in Headington was in piles on the sides of the footpaths. What we country dwellers had to put up with! On the way home the single lane through the drifts was just a 'white out' with driven snow and we nearly became stuck several times, but fortunately we kept going and with luck did not meet another vehicle coming the other way. Ours was the last car through that day as shortly after we heard that the road was again blocked.

During the heavy fall of snow in the early 1970's, fortunately not lasting more than a few days, Eric the milkman managed to serve his customers by dragging the deliveries around the village on a toboggan, truly a Herculean effort!

If we ever have other winters like 1947 and 1962/63, many of our new parishioners are in for a shock! Perhaps all those people buying 4 wheel drive vehicles know something the rest of us don't ?

A Christmas Journey 1926   By Hector Wheeler

A story of another spell of bad weather written by my father that involved me at a very early age, needless to say I don't remember much about it !

In early December 1926 my mother asked us to spend Christmas with her at Garsington, so my wife and I and our five month old son arrived there on Christmas Eve. When we awoke on Christmas morning there was a very sharp frost and a strong easterly wind, it then started to snow and by midday was a howling blizzard. Boxing day came and deep snow was everywhere with most roads blocked by drifts. After three days we heard that the road to Cowley, Headington and the

Bayswater Road was clear ,so we decided to go home and we left Garsington about noon.

At that time I had a motor bike and sidecar. We progressed without any trouble until about two miles from Beckley when the bike became stuck, and we could see that there was no way through as the road had not been cleared. We struggled and got the bike free and after parking it in a nearby farm shed started to walk the rest of the way home. It was quite an effort with the baby and a heavy suitcase to carry, but we eventually reached a house I was building in New Inn Road that we called the stone bungalow (now Greystones). We went in and lit a fire, my wife fed the baby, we thawed out and rested for about an hour.

Half a mile to go, and in darkness lit only by the whiteness of the snow which in places was over five feet deep, we finally got to Church Street almost exhausted, to find the doors, windows and sideway of our house covered by a wall of snow which I had to dig out before we could get inside. Once inside however a fire, some hot food and a warm bed soon made us feel far more comfortable and so thankful to be home. A journey that would usually take about half an hour had taken us well over seven hours.

Two weeks later I was able to bring my bike home and get back to work as normal. I shall ever forget that journey from Garsington to Beckley in Christmas week 1926.

Hector Wheeler 1970

Our forebears suffered extremes of weather. Things have not changed that much, except that today we hear about it on radio, and see it on television almost as it happens.

Chapter Ten

Beckley at Play

Beckley has always been proud of its sporting prowess, having cricket and football teams for over seventy years. Games were regularly played, as you will read below with the bare necessities of equipment and certainly not ideal pitches to play on. Nevertheless over the years a great deal of enjoyment was obtained not only by the players but by the organisers and spectators, and there was always the pub to celebrate a win or drown your sorrows after losing a game.

The Boys Club   by Hector Wheeler

In 1932 we had a new vicar the Revd Edgar Millen, he soon settled in and was well liked because of his quiet and courteous manner. One of his first ideas was to form a boys club which in spite of a lot of effort, was not to become a success for the following reasons. He asked me to help set up the club and we raised enough money to buy a football and timber to make goalposts. I made the goalposts and one Saturday morning, with help from other men and boys from the village, set them up and marked out the pitch in Farmer Tomkins field near the White House. On arriving at the field that afternoon for what was to be our first match, we found to our dismay that someone had removed the goalposts and despite all our efforts to find them not one clue was ever found.

The following summer we bought some cricket bats and other gear to enable us to play cricket. The Women's Institute gave us permission to store them in their room at the Grove, but a week or so later they too disappeared and like the

Beckley Cricket mid 1920's outside The Abingdon Arms

goalposts were never found.

We used the W.I. room for our club evenings and by kind offers obtained table tennis and billiard tables. There was insufficient space for storing these large items in the W.I. room and when not in use they were put in one of the potato storerooms at the back of Grove Farm cartshed. These rooms were under the stables of Grove House and were very damp which wasn't very good for the tables. As it happened however it did not much matter, for only a short time after they too vanished! Someone either did not want Beckley Boys Club to succeed or thought that their own needs were greater than ours.

The vicar then had an idea to start what was called 'The

Beckley and Horton Dramatic Society'. To raise money we held social evenings and whist drives and it was decided to embark on a production of 'Cinderella.' I was made stage manager and prop maker and we had a major problem with how to make the fairy coach. After trying many things we eventually decided on using an old pram with two small boys dressed as horses. The Fairy Queen then produced them out of a large cardboard box. After the night of the performance the play was voted a great success - until we counted the takings and found that the income didn't cover the expenses. Several more social evenings were held - but no more plays.

The Revd Edgar Millen left the village in 1936 to take up an appointment at Wells Cathedral. As he was very well liked nearly everyone in the village was sorry to see him go.

Hector Wheeler 1972

The next two articles describe cricket and football in the village before and following the Second World War and leading to the eventual purchase of the playing field and the first pavilion. Money as always was a problem and the pitches were still a challenge, but as you will read things were gradually getting better.

Village Sport   by Malcolm Sumner

The field between the Common Road and Cookes Copse belonging to Grove House is where the Beckley cricket team played their matches before the Second World War. The team included Bernard Gatz (the village bakers son), Bernard Grace, my uncle Frank Sumner (fast bowler) and my father Ted. The pitch on this sloping field was not very good and there were no changing facilities. After the war a football team was formed and meant a new pitch had to be found. For a while games were played on Otmoor next to the RAF tower and members of the Air Force played their part in the village teams of the 1950's. One of them R Hart (Lofty to his friends) played at centre-half for the football team and was a fearsome fast bowler, he once dismissed the whole of the Horton-cum-Studley team for eleven runs of which six were byes!

The next move was to the field next to the White House by permission of the then farmer Mr Tomkins of New Inn Farm. Grass mowing was by a herd of Jersey cows which meant that pancakes had to be cleared up before play could commence. The changing room was an old wooden henhouse and a cold water cattle trough was there if you wanted to clean off. The football team played in the Jersey League and wore red and white stripes, white shorts and red socks. Travelling to away games was in the back of a removal van leaving from

Beckley Cricket Club, early 1950's

outside the village pub.

The cricket pitch had a lot of work put into it and compared with other village pitches of those days it was very good. Matches were played against other local villages and teams from the University. Talk was then of the village buying their own ground and a fund to collect £1000 was started, dances and other fund raising efforts were held before at long last Beckley had its own sports field on the present site. For the first cricket match on the new ground an old bell tent was used for changing and a year later Mr Lankester obtained the first pavilion which had changing rooms, showers and a large

Beckley Football Club 1958-59

hall for teas, receptions and other village functions.

In 1958 at a meeting in the Abingdon Arms a new football team was formed under the management of Tom Sumner. We entered the Cuddesdon League and players had to reside within three miles of the village. The colours were

Red shirts with white sleeves, White shorts, and red socks. The first match was played against Chinnor Reserves with the result 6 -1 to Beckley. The team on that memorable day was ; K.Williams, D.Williams, B.Williams, J.Wilson, I. Scarrot, D. Brewerton, G.Skidmore, G.Lee, D.Shaw, M.Sumner, J. Bedding and F. Mortby. The manager Tom Sumner was to be a stalwart for the club for many years to follow.

Malcolm Sumner 1998

Our Village Cricket by Bill Quartermain

Cricket was a regular feature here in Beckley on summer Sunday afternoons. At first the matches were played in a field on Otmoor Lane but when the present field was acquired it was fantastic, for the first time we had a flat field to play on! The men would gather on Sunday morning with hand mowers and the roller to prepare the wicket, mark out the pitch and set the stumps, I don't think we had any bails at that time. ˙

After Sunday lunch village families wives and children came to watch the match. They brought blankets to sit on in the shade of the hedge, and baskets of sandwiches, cakes and lemonade with flasks of tea, everything then home-made of course.

The pavilion was a wooden hut where we padded up, there were three sets of pads, one for the wicket keeper and the others for the batsmen. We tended to wear only one pad whilst batting, one could run faster between the wickets that way. There were two bats, the man who was out would hand the bat to the man coming in. The scoreboard consisted of a black board with nails on the front on which to hang the numbered squares to show the score, wickets down and so on,

136

and kept up to date by one of the older children.

No one had any whites to wear but eventually we all had blue caps (I've still got mine!) we wore grey flannel trousers and plimsolls on our feet. I usually wore my trilby hat except when batting which as a rule wasn't for very long. We did not wear helmets, face guards, or boxes to protect ourselves or need to whiten our faces like circus clowns, we played for the love of the sport.

The match would usually finish by 7.00pm which was opening time in the pub and we all gathered there for a cricket tea. The women and children in the garden and the men in the bar to play darts, dominoes, aunt sally, crib etc and enjoy a pint of beer, a very nice social gathering of village folk. After the Oddfellows barn was pulled down the pub was the only meeting place in the village.

Bill Quartermain 1998

Beckley Cricket Club 1988

Cuttings from the Oxford Mail.

The actual dates are unknown but from the players names mentioned it was in the early 1980's.

Beckley Sports Football Club circa 1980
Reproduced by kind permission of Oxford and County Newspapers.

"It seems I was a little premature in these notes last week, when Division 1 Beckley Sports were praised for fulfilling all their fixtures in the right spirit, despite losing all twenty of their league matches. Alas due to a mix up when the secretary took a holiday, Beckley were unable to raise a side for games against Blackbird ASC Reserves and Viking Sports and they were fined and forfeited the points."

"Playing his first game for Beckley in the competition, Mark Surman made no mistake from a good pass from Peter

138

Wheeler who also had a hand in the second goal, although this time not a role he relished. Wheeler was brought crashing down in the penalty area by a Blackbird Leys defender and Peter Surman converted to give Beckley a 2 - 0 win."

"After a string of poor results in the league, Beckley Sports returned to form with a 2 - 0 victory over Oxford University Press Reserves in the quarter final replay of the Supplementary Cup. Beckley led by a single goal through Dave Wilding at half time. The printers came into the game more in the second half and only the woodwork prevented an equaliser. Skipper Pete Wheeler then made the game safe for Beckley with a shot that spun out of the keeper's hands and into the net to put them into their second cup semi-final."

Can I please point out that the Peter Wheeler referred to is not me but my son - all very confusing!

In 1973 Brian Westbury started a Youth Club that was to prove a most successful and long lasting venture. Early meetings were held in the W.I. room. Some time afterwards Grove House was sold, and for a time the club was without a home. Enquiries were made about hiring the school hall but the idea came to nothing when the rental fee quoted was more than the club could afford. From 1982 onwards the club was able to set up a permanent home in the new Village Hall. The range of activities undertaken over the years was enormous as was the popularity of the club indicated by its bulging membership boosted by youngsters from neighbouring villages. The long period of successful operation can best be summed up by Brian himself in an article from the Beckley Newsletter in 1994 just prior to his retirement after twenty one years as Beckley Youth Club Leader.

The Youth Club   by Brian Westbury

Twenty one years is a long time to be involved in voluntary youth work and I have decided to hang up my table tennis bat, pool cue, darts, rounders bat, not forgetting my tour operators hat, to make way for new and younger blood in September 1994.

Beckley Youth Club, a sponsored cycle event.

It has been a wonderful experience being Beckley Youth Club leader for so many years and I know that our four children Catherine, Duncan, Rebecca and Louisa have gained an incredible education on how to manage a youth club! The membership presently stands at forty eight, although two years ago it was sixty three. I have glorious memories of the last twenty one years. The club started in the reading room adjacent to the church and Grove House, I recall that the most popular record we played in 1973 was Gary Glitter singing 'Come On, Come On'. My fondest memories are of the parties which were held at Christmas for all the Senior Citizens in our village, a great deal of effort was needed and provided by the youth members in catering, waiting at tables and providing entertainment, as well of course as raising the money for the parties.

Over the years I believe that the numbers 1 to 90 are well instilled in my mind after so much Bingo calling! The roads to Oasis Leisure Centre, Alton Towers, American Adventure Park, Oxford Ice Rink, Grasshoppers and London are so well known to me I believe if I was blindfolded I could direct a coach driver to any of these places, not forgetting suitable burger, fish and chips and service stations on route!

'MC' Brian Westbury & Amanda Sumner

Many 'outsiders' believe that running a youth club throughout the year is just setting aside Friday nights from six to ten. Quite clearly this is not the case, only half my time is spent actually attending Youth Club evenings, one must not forget the preparation time in buying confectionery and drinks, organising outings, membership paperwork, posters, diaries, work associated with local organisations, weekly banking and attending Area Youth Committee meetings. I look forward to having my Friday evenings free to 'get into the garden' or turn a fruit bowl on my lathe, however, I will surely miss the calls of " Come on Mr Westbury let me beat you at Pool - Connect 4 - draughts.............," or " When is our next outing Brian?" I sincerely hope our village can find a replacement Youth Leader as soon as possible and that all our efforts and hard work in setting up the Club some twenty one years ago will not be lost.

Finally I must say thank you to Peter Gibbons, Anne Ratford, Tim Ratford, Gordon Thomas, David Prosser and a very big thank you from the bottom of my heart to Mrs Pether and Steve Dewhurst, not forgetting the support I have received from my wife Gill and our children because without them all Beckley would not have become one of the finest and most respected Clubs in Oxfordshire. To the members of the Youth Club - all I can say is please support and help your new Leader in every way possible and maintain Beckley Youth Club as one of the top clubs in the County.

Brian Westbury 1994

The magnificent legacy left by Brian Westbury for the youth of Beckley and its neighbouring villages has been taken up and carried on by Anne Purse. It is difficult to know how this woman finds time to do all the things she is involved in, as the poet Virgil once said "We can't all do everything" but Anne is the exception, she certainly tries and what's more usually succeeds. The Youth Club is going strong and prospects are bright way into the twenty first century.

The Tennis Club

In 1991 a tennis hard court was built on the playing field largely due to the generosity of Arthur Cooke. A club was formed which for several years was keenly supported, unfortunately enthusiasm has since waned and at the time of writing (1999) efforts are being made to revitalise the club and refurbish the court.

Arthur Cooke officiating at the opening of the new court, 1991

Coronation 1953

Oddfellows Parade

Chapter Eleven

Tillers of the Soil

Of all the changes that have occurred in our village within living memory, the evolution or perhaps nearer revolution, that has taken place on the farms has probably been the most significant. The great improvements in crop yields brought about by the use of plants bred to produce higher output and be less susceptible to weather damage has greatly increased arable efficiency. On the other hand increased use of artificial fertilisers, pesticides and herbicides has since brought criticism about their use, but no one can deny that the farmers filled the nations larders during times when it was really needed. Farmers today are being blamed for the disappearance of many forms of wildlife by grubbing out hedges, ploughing up headlands, and for the effects of the use of artificial fertilisers and herbicides which do not discriminate between crops and wild flowers, and pesticides which kill off the insects on which many animals and birds depend for food. The success of the nature reserve surrounding the Rifle Range has been largely attributed to the absence of nitrate and phosphate pollutants in the area. We in Beckley have probably not suffered as badly as many areas, but nevertheless it cannot be denied we have far fewer birds today compared with days past. However I do think it unfair to heap all the blame on to the farmers, they were only doing what successive governments have over the years, encouraged them to do. Much is said today about going back to basics, e. g. Organic farming, this is an admirable sentiment but with lower crop yields it is difficult to see how such methods could possibly feed our burgeoning population.

Ted Hall's Oxfordshire waggon drawing up Otmoor Lane in the early 1920's

In the early years of the 20th century, there were a great many farms and smallholdings in the parish supporting a large number of families, most of the mainly static population of those days earning their living from the land. Farms were then entirely dependent on the farm labourer and the horse to carry out the work, necessitating long hours of arduous heavy tasks. I recall Bill Hudson, who lived in what is now Otmoor Cottage in Church Street, telling me that in the summer, he would go to the Abingdon Arms just after dawn to fill a stone jar with a gallon of beer to sustain him whilst using a scythe to cut hay on Otmoor, usually not returning home until after dusk. In a wet season haymaking would often not be completed and had to be abandoned in November! In addition to the seasonal harvests, there were always the ongoing jobs of livestock to tend and feed and cows to milk, all by hand. With no water on tap for washing down and for the stock, it all had to be hand pumped or drawn up from the nearest well and then carried to the point of use.

After the first World War, changes gradually began, mowing machines, threshing boxes, all kinds of machines for the preparation of feedstuffs and most importantly of all, steam engines and tractors started to appear, albeit quite basic machines which never the less was the beginning of the replacement of the horse as the main means of transport and power. The advent of farm mechanisation meant that fewer men were needed as labourers and this trend was to continue up to the time of and after the Second World War. It was fortunate indeed that the period generally co-incided with the establishment of the Cowley car factories which took up much of the unwanted labour from the farms, together with the population becoming more mobile and able to travel to work away from the village by means of bicycles, motorcycles and eventually cars.

The tendency since the Second World War has been that when farms become vacant due to retirement or death, the houses are sold to private buyers, and barns and outbuildings converted in to dwellings, the land being taken over by other farms. Consequently many of the old Beckley farming family names have disappeared. In latter years due to over production and falling prices, a lot due I suspect, to European Union intervention, farmers have had to diversify their efforts into extra ways of making a living. So we now have among the normal agricultural activities, farmyard industrial sites, farm shops, 'pick your own' fields of fruit and vegetables, wildlife reserves and touring caravan sites. Very different, but economically necessary circumstances to those prevailing a hundred years ago.

Modern farm machinery is sophisticated, efficient and - expensive, and in terms of what can be achieved with minimum labour, very necessary. Probably the most incredible fact is that in little more than seventy years we have progressed from working the farms by human effort and single or multiple animal horsepower, to today's monster machines producing 120 or more horsepower. The machines do seem to get bigger and bigger and have difficulty in manoeuvring through the village especially past the ever growing number of parked cars in streets virtually unchanged from the days of the horses and carts. With these modern monsters however, advantage can be taken of the weather so that ploughing, harvesting etc can be done swiftly and efficiently at the right time. But having said that, working the land is still, and probably always will be a never ending battle with Mother nature who can never be taken for granted, and usually manages to play a few tricks when least expected!

I often hear adverse comments about noises and smells emanating from farm animals and farming activities and complaints about mud deposited on the roads by farm vehicles, but if you choose to live in the country you must be prepared to put up with such things, that is all part of country life, be grateful for all its benefits and enjoy it.

So much for a non farmers view of the agricultural scene, (but I am country born and bred) now read what the farmers have to say.

Lower Farm   by David Talbot

I came to Lower Farm at the start of 1960 expecting to move on in a year or so. Forty years later I find myself still here. It was in November 1959 that I first saw Lower Farm on a foul day and from the bottom of Church Street, having taken the wrong turn at the Church. The place had been empty for some time and the land was running wild, the RAF bomb disposal team having only recently completed the checking required to allow the land to be farmed again following use during the war of the adjacent bombing range. The house and buildings appeared derelict a pretty depressing picture from a farming point of view, but there was something special about the place that I have never been able to identify clearly. Now years later having escaped the ravages of progress - at one point it was going to be demolished to make way for the M40 and then flooded by the proposed Otmoor reservoir - it is much easier to appreciate why it is such a pleasant place to live.

With the rashness of youth I decided to take the farm and moved in during January 1960. There was no electricity or water and no loo, over halfway through the 20th century and only 50 miles from London! The electricity and sanitation took six months but I had a telephone in seven days and I remember it sitting in the middle of the table as the only concession to the modern world. One of the first farmers I met was Joe Tompkins who farmed dairy cows with his father at New Inn Farm. I recall him telling me that I would not last long as the place was un-farmable, nobody had ever stayed there very long. About twenty years later in the Abingdon Arms I reminded him of what he had said, by this time we were good friends, Joe was one of natures true gentlemen and was overcome with embarrassment. He spent the rest of the evening buying my beer. Joes father was a great character and always insisted on being allowed to castrate the young piglets which was almost a weekly event at that time. He would arrive, take out a used double sided Blue Gillette razor blade from a match box, wrap a bit of cardboard round one side and proceed to castrate pigs quicker than we could catch them. The removed parts were thrown over his shoulder where the collie always positioned himself at the sound of the first squeal. Not much sign of Health and Safety Inspectors then.

On Boxing night in 1962 it snowed and for the next seven weeks it was impossible to get to the village except across the fields by tractor, the village was also cut off from Headington from time to time and the milk arrived on hand drawn sledge on occasion. It was exceptionally cold and feeding and particularly getting water to the 350 in-lamb ewes was a daily battle. I ended up having them in the garden and yard and remember them looking down through the windows into the house the frozen snow was so deep. Fortunately it thawed before lambing which took place then outside with huge losses of lambs just due to exposure, so unlike the modern indoor lambing pens.

During a very hot spell of weather in my first summer here, I was wandering around looking for some escaped bullocks, quite a regular job due to the poor state of the fences. It was one of those heavy humid Otmoor days and I was having great difficulty resisting the urge to sit down and go to sleep. Breaking through a thick hedge I was confronted with the sight of Beckley Park. I was completely unaware of its existence, the approaching thunder storm and the eerie silence apart from the buzzing of hundreds of insects was a weird experience. The doors and windows were all open but not a soul about and I wondered if I had stepped back into the past. I carried on up the hill to Upper Park Farm still looking for the cattle and met Jack Wakelin for the first time who said not to fuss about the straying stock as they would turn up sometime! He offered me a glass of water and on entering the house I saw a tree growing in the kitchen and on up through the roof. Quite an afternoon, and I realised when I got home without the bullocks (which did indeed turn up in a few days) that I had some pretty unconventional neighbours.

Towards the end of the sixties saw the 'reclamation' of Otmoor and I am glad I had no part in it. It seems incredible today that the destruction of this unique piece of wet moorland was a matter of no concern ,and so now thirty years later huge sums of money are being spent to recreate what was destroyed. Sadly it will take several hundred years to return to the place I remember, very wild ,isolated and absolutely teeming with wildlife. During the sixties and early seventies I drained most of the land but resisted the removal of all the hedgerows, although the sixty acres adjoining Otmoor which was divided into 19 fields just had to have some truly giant hedges taken out. In 1966 I installed a pump system of drainage which was designed by a Dutchman and has worked successfully now for 35 years.

One morning just after the Great Train Robbery police appeared everywhere and I was asked endless questions. I could not understand why they were so interested in me and the farm buildings, however it transpired that a mailbag had been reported found at the bottom of Otmoor Lane. Needless to say it had nothing to do with the robbery. I have often wondered what I would have done had I found a bag of used notes!

The second half of the twentieth century has seen huge changes in farming and also to the villages. Ted Hall told me that at haymaking before the war there would have been a gang of thirty men cutting hay on the lower fields, there has been no employed labour here since 1968. The size of machinery and the speed with which the work can now be done has decimated the number of people involved in farming, at harvest now we can do in one hour what took at least a day 30 years ago. Consequently Beckley is no longer a farming orientated village and people living, but not working in it sometimes have difficulty grasping the concept of the countryside as a workplace for the remaining farmers. I shudder to think of the reaction if we were to drive 50 beef cows with their calves through the village twice a year as we did in the past. I have even been asked why tractors have to use the road!

It is difficult to predict the role of the farmer in the country in the next century but I suspect that it will be more as a park keeper than as a food producer. Only the passing of another century, let alone a millennium, will reveal if that is good or bad.

Talbot of Otmoor 1999

*Ted Hall haymaking in Church Ground.. Lower Farm is off the picture
to the left. 1935-36.*

John Cox is now one of only a handful of farmers left in
Beckley and is certainly the longest serving. Like David
Talbot he too lived at Lower Farm. This is his story in his own
words.

Over Seventy Years on the Farm   by John Cox

I came to Beckley with my family as a small boy in
September 1926 to Lower Farm. At this time Beckley and the
surrounding villages had no milk delivery service, so instead
of taking the milk to Oxford on a wholesale basis, my father
started a retail round. The milk was delivered in a two and a
half gallon bucket and was measured into customers jugs with
either a pint or half pint measure. The milk was sold at 2½d (a
fraction over 1p) a pint and eggs at 6d (2 ½p) a dozen.

For two years, until we moved up to Folly Farm, my two elder sisters and I walked up through the fields to school. The milk round was carried on and when at fourteen years of age I left school, I took over the running of it. This continued until milk was rationed during World War II. We were encouraged by the Government to increase production to meet extra demand and I sold the retail round and returned to the wholesale market.

When the war started in 1939 farmers were called upon to plough up the grass fields to grow the maximum amount of corn. A large proportion of Folly Farm and Common Farm were semi-derelict as a result of the 1930's depression. To help produce more corn, my father and myself together with a good friend Harry Newell armed with slashers and one tractor and helped by longer evenings brought about by double summertime, reclaimed a good proportion of the land.

In 1942 after having my right arm smashed in an altercation with a bull, I spent a month in hospital listening to the air raid sirens and eating dried egg for breakfast, which I believe came from America under the lease-lend agreement.

There are still visible signs of two German bomb craters in Otmoor Lane which fell just short of the homes of Ziba Sumner and Jesse Frost, Jesse for some reason always kept his bedroom light on during the black-out.

In 1943 I became tenant of part of Grove Farm which included the barn now converted into living accommodation. The barn was used to store corn and potatoes until 1977 when I purchased the land and relinquished the tenancy of the barn and yard.

After returning to wholesale milk production, I met my wife, a farmers daughter from Bedfordshire. She obtained a degree in the dairy industry and held a management position in the then Ministry of Agriculture, Fisheries and Food up to the time we were married. I give her great credit for the progress we have made at Folly Farm. After college training our two sons have taken over where we left off, we have full confidence in them for the future.

John Cox 1997

(*Folly Farm was identified on a map dated 1797 as Whistlers Folly.*)

Farmers children are often thought to lead idyllic lives, this may be true in some cases probably more so today, but between the two World Wars farming was not a very prosperous occupation, and life was often bereft of other than the very basic essentials. Phyllis however, with the optimism of youth seemed to cope quite well.

Childhood at Grove Farm   by Phyllis Wheeler

I spent my early years living with my parents in the house at the top of Church Lane. It is now known as Grove Farm House but up to 1964 the farmhouse was what is now called Nokewood House, occupied by my great uncle Ted Hall who ran the farm with my father. Our house had very little in the way of creature comforts, no bathroom, all ablutions carried out in the scullery in summer and in front of the kitchen range (which was also used for cooking) in winter. The water was heated by kettles on the fire (no electricity until after 1936) or in the big coal heated copper in the scullery which also boiled the weekly wash, all the water had to be

155

pumped from the well down at the farmhouse and carried up in buckets. There was no central heating and I'm sure my bedroom windows stayed frosted up all through the winter! The toilet was a chilly outside privy halfway down the garden. Due to the close proximity of the farmyard in summer we always had lots of flies. In those days the usual way to dispose of them was by the use of 'fly papers', they were strips of sticky paper that were hung from the ceiling. In quite a short time they were black with stuck on flies and had to be regularly replaced.

Father hand milked the cows mornings and evenings in the cowhouse, (now a house called 'The Shippen'). He sat on a three legged stool and wore an old trilby hat the front of which

Grove Farm as it was.

was thick with grease where he pushed his head against the cows flanks to make them stand still. Uncle Ted and his wife Aunt Kate sold milk and butter from the farmhouse, the dairy was a long narrow north facing room that was always cool (no refrigeration then of course). The milk was placed in large shallow pans which enabled the cream to be skimmed off the top ready to be churned into butter. We kept pigs and chickens in the yard at Common Farm (now a dwelling) and grew vegetables in the garden of what is now 'High Corner House'. Virtual self-sufficiency in fruit and vegetables, with the added bonus of pork, bacon and eggs helped enormously during the period of rationing in World War Two, but it was never easy, continual hard work was necessary for the results to be enjoyed.

There were always plenty of places to play on the farm, and in the fields and orchards, and at one time whilst climbing in the sycamore trees in Home Close (now the school grounds), I got well and truly stuck, unable to get up or down. My cries for help were heard by Farmer Franklin from Noke riding by on his grey horse on his way to enjoy a whisky with Uncle Ted, he rode up close to the tree and lifted me down on to his horse, with nothing hurt except my pride. I remember clearly one Christmas eve, there was a knock on the door and Mr Willis the Carrier stood there with a large box he had brought from Oxford railway station. Inside was a present, a dolls pram sent from my relatives at Lincoln.

Phyllis Wheeler (Formerly Phyllis Senior) 1999

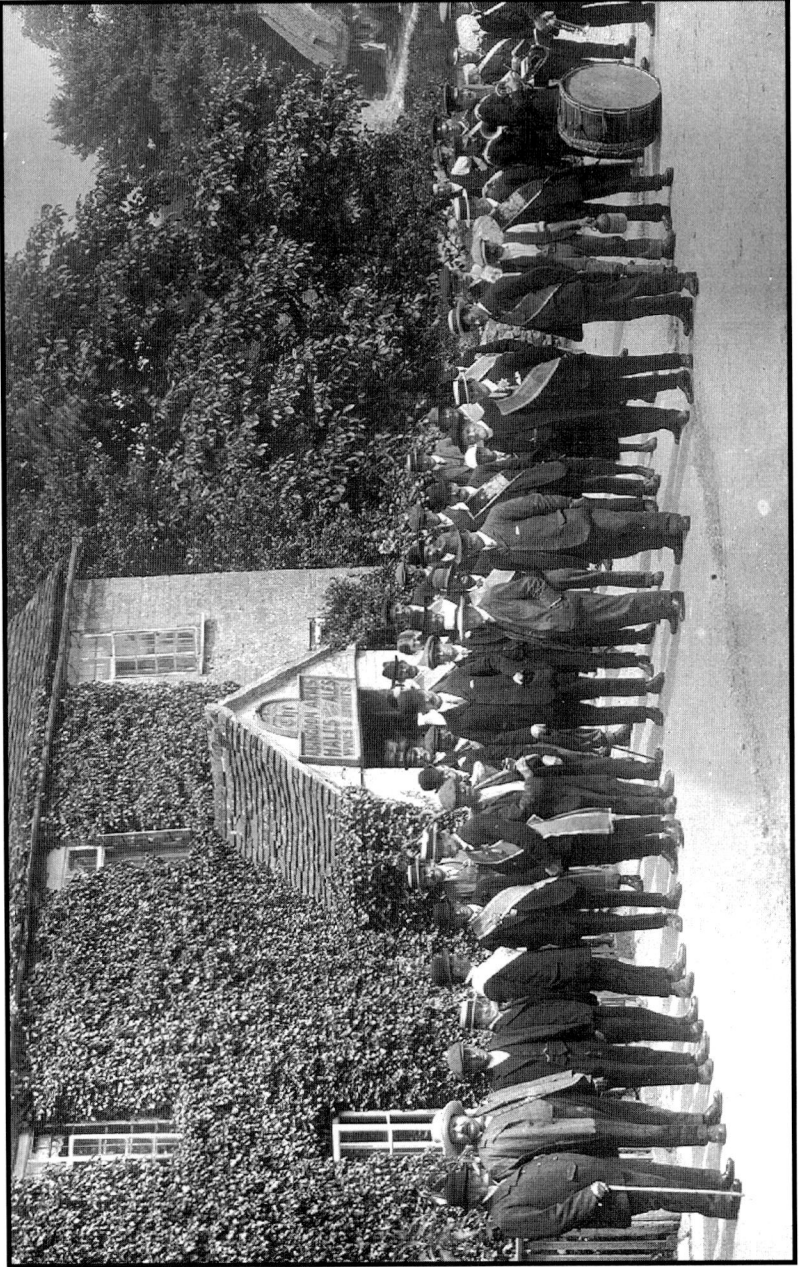

'Oddfellows' gathering outside the Abingdon Arms.

Chapter Twelve

The Village Hall

The first idea of providing a village hall was mentioned at a Church Council meeting in 1937. At that time grants were available for new buildings or conversion of existing premises, The Hon Mr Holland-Hibbert had offered to give a piece of land for a new hall, and it was also suggested that two existing buildings be inspected with a view to conversion. One, the old carpenters and coffin makers sawing shop in Otmoor Lane owned by Mr Fielding, (now converted into a dwelling called Cripps Barn) was looked at and found to be unsuitable. The other, the old Oddfellows Barn opposite the Abingdon Arms and next to Shipley Cottage, was considered a possibility and Mr Holland-Hibbert offered to buy and give the building to the village if sufficient support was forthcoming to make the scheme a success, and it was decided to approach the owner, Lady Tweedsmuir to see if it could be purchased. Meanwhile plans were drawn up for both converting the barn and a new building. No decision was reached and it was then decided to refer the matter to the Parish Council. Perhaps a logical decision but as it was mostly the same people serving on both Councils it probably made very little difference.

In 1938 the Parish Council discussed the matter on the

159

same lines as the PCC and it was decided that if there was sufficient support forthcoming from the village they would go ahead with whichever scheme was favoured. No further mention was made in the Council Minutes presumably because of the moratorium on new projects brought about by the outbreak of the Second World War, until ten years later in 1948 the Parish Meeting proposed that a Playing Field/ Recreation Ground be purchased. The proposed piece of land was on Woodperry Road and the owners Oxfordshire County Council agreed to sell or lease 5 to 6 acres for parish use. In the meantime the Oddfellows Barn with its adjacent old farm buildings, had reached a very bad state of repair and was eventually pulled down to make way for two new houses.

Over the next few years protracted negotiations were carried on with various authorities, and in 1952 the Parish Council decided against raising a loan of £250.00 to purchase the land but that a Recreation Ground Committee be asked to elect trustees to carry out the project, so absolving the Parish from responsibility. It was suggested that the Council would consider the matter further when this Committee had raised £100. The Committee however by holding whist drives, dances etc raised the money and Beckley at last had it's playing field, and now thoughts turned again towards the provision of a hall/sports pavilion.

At this point Jack Lankester takes up the story.

The 'First' Village Hall   by Jack Lankester

My first wife , Patricia, and I came to live in Beckley in 1954, and in the course of the next few years gradually became involved in local activities. At that time, England had

160

a successful cricket team and everyone in the village was keen to revive the local cricket team. The acquisition of the playing field at last made this realisable. Much work was needed to get the ground in order and to prepare a pitch, all done by the enthusiasts themselves. I remember well the weekly agony of getting my big Ransome lawnmower up there with the help of Tom Sumner, the indefatigable club secretary. It soon became apparent that if the club was to succeed it must have a

The 'first' village hall reproduced from a rather blurred photograph

pavilion, which would be used for other team games as well.

At this time the University was at the start of great expansion, and as Surveyor to the University I was responsible for the management of its major building programme. One of the projects in this programme which was scheduled to start in 1958/59 was the multiple library building, now known as the St Cross building in Manor Road. The site was leased to the Territorial Army who were housed in a motley collection of wooden huts, first erected during the 1914-18 war, and brought back to extensive use in 1939-45.

During the clearance of the site, one of these tired and elderly huts found its way to Beckley, where the demolition contractors who had removed it laid a concrete base, and with help from village enthusiasts re-constructed it on the playing field more or less on the site of the present building. Over a period of several months it was made ready for use, I will try to describe it. The foundation was a concrete slab which also served as the floor. This was painted with a dark reddish-brown floor paint to stop the concrete dusting; the walls were timber framed, weather boarded on the outside and lined internally with fibreboard. There was no insulation, which was still an uncommon concept in those days. The roof was a very low double pitch, covered with tarred roofing felt. Simple lavatories, showers and a sink were screened off at one end and a septic tank dug nearby. Electricity for lighting and heating was installed and overhead infra-red heating panels, which had become redundant on some other University building site, were put in. The finished building was eighteen feet wide and seventy feet long.

Given the modest expectations of the time, and the even more modest resources then available it was a great success, not only because it immediately made possible a range of activities which would otherwise been impossible, but because it was a symbol -- an indicator of what could be achieved, even in a small community with enthusiasm and determination. Potential cricketers and footballers took part in the building work and many more were involved in raising funds. This took all the traditional forms, notably village fetes. On one occasion Alan Bullock opened proceedings and on another Tim Rice, Andrew Lloyd Webber's partner and lyricist, and a keen cricketer, joined in. On an earlier occasion hydrogen balloons were set off with the help of the Clarendon

Laboratory. One balloon I remember, reached East Germany with its supplicatory message. The Parish Council had very limited funds(the parish was much less prosperous then) and fearful of a never-ending commitment if things went wrong, gave its blessing but no cash.

During the 1950's Parish Meetings and Parish Council meetings were held, by permission of the Women's Institute, in what was called the WI Room - originally one of the classrooms of the old school attached to Grove House. This shared arrangement was not always satisfactory particularly for large gatherings, or when both bodies wanted it at the same time. The pavilion was then brought into use and its status raised to that of Village Hall. Relations between the WI and the Parish Council were always good and the only friction I can recall was over where to keep the 36 chairs that belonged to the village. Before the hall was built they had been kept in the WI room. The Parish Council took the view that since they belonged to the village their proper home was in the hall, although it was happy for the WI to have the use of them when needed, so long as they brought them back. This meant moving chairs back and forth all the time - a frightful fag. Amazingly it took several years to work out a solution, which at the time seemed like the wisdom of Solomon. This was to allocate 18 chairs to the WI to keep in their room and 18 to the Parish Council to keep in the hall, borrowing from each other's stock when numbers required.

If the "new" building had shown what could be done, its deficiencies were always apparent and became more and more irksome as time went on. Looking back it seems quite amazing that it remained in active use for so long. It was ugly, gloomy and uncomfortable and had a definite character and a will to survive (rather like Grandma in those old Giles cartoons), which sorely tested the temper, patience, and enthusiasm of those who had to look after it. But even its deficiencies had some positive merit. I always thought the system of overhead heating had a moderating effect on decisions taken at meetings. The participants always started with hot heads, but invariably finished up with cold feet.

So I raise my glass to the old village hall, and "All who sailed in her!"

Jack Lankester. 1999.

The 'New' Hall

Following the Silver Jubilee celebrations in 1977 it was realised that the village sorely needed a new hall and a small ad-hoc committee canvassed the parish and village organisations to determine the level of support for such a venture.

With the backing of Beckley Sports and Social Club who badly needed new changing facilities, many authorities and organisations were contacted for grants and/or loans.

It was then suggested that in order to encompass the wider village aspect a Village Hall Steering Committee be formed consisting of members of all the interested parties. Under the Chairmanship of Brian Westbury negotiations were started with a firm supplying second hand sectional buildings and fund raising ventures went ahead, all under the watchful eye of the Parish Council. It is amazing that with all the statutory, financial, legal and charitable items involved in what would appear to be a simple project, that everything went reasonably smoothly, there were 'hiccups' of course but all ably dealt with by the Steering Committee and its Chairman.

Continuous fund raising went on in the form of coffee mornings and bring and buy sales held in various homes in the village. A fancy dress football match, men versus women was held on Boxing Day. Sponsorship raised by Rod Dawber and Brian Greatbatch successfully running the first London Marathon in 1981. A dance/supper held in Holton Village Hall, catering by Beckley ladies. Car cleaning and sales of wood kindling by Charles and Ced Barbour. Donations by various members of the community.

The project was estimated to cost in the region of £12000. At this juncture the steering committee had raised just over £1000 which together with grants from SODC of £4000 and £3000 from the Parish Council left a shortfall of £4000. It was anticipated that the Committee would raise

Excavations for the new hall started in 1980, the old hall is in the background.

another £1000 so a loan of £3000 was sought and negotiated with the SODC to be repaid at the rate of £600 per annum for five years.

In 1981 the hall building sections were delivered and work commenced with many residents giving free help with the ground work, erection and fitting particularly Mick Bennett, Pete Gibbons, Brian Westbury (including the architectural work), Mark Girdler, John Higginson, Ced Barbour and George Bowerman.

The necessity for money raising continued to dominate and in March 1984 the 150 Club was set up to repay the £600 per annum due to SODC. Since the loan was cleared the club has been a valuable source of income for the ongoing and seemingly ever increasing costs incurred by the Hall.

The Hall consisted of a main function room and a fitted kitchen, a committee room, male and female toilets, and "Home and Away" changing rooms each complete with two showers. The old derelict wooden building having served its purpose for many years, was sold for £25 and removed from the site.

The Beckley Village Hall project was entered for the Oxfordshire Rural Community Council's Village Ventures Competition in 1982 .... and won !

Oxford Mail Report. May 1982

First prize of £200 in this years Village Ventures Competition to promote community enterprise has been won by Beckley. The judges say that the village - along with other award winners - has shown what can be done with imagination and a lot of hard work.

Beckley's entry was on behalf of the village hall project which started off when the football club needed new changing facilities. It was then decided to build a joint sports and village hall and an old prefab building was acquired and renovated .A Youth Club has been re-formed, and an Over 60's club is now planned.

The Newsletter

An enterprise that has proved to be a valued spin off from the effort of providing the new hall was the launching of the Village Newsletter. Started by Brian Westbury and called 'Village Hall News' the early copies were intended to publicise the village hall building progress and fund raising activities, it was then wisely decided to widen its scope to cover all aspects of life in the village, it was renamed 'Beckley News' with the editorship taken over by Arthur Cooke who published it until 1989. There was then a period when no copies were produced until 1992 when the paper was started up again by Nigel Purse and renamed 'Beckley Parish Newsletter'. Nigel was editor until 1996 when Peter Wheeler (senior) took over. All the editorial and other input together with the distribution is provided on a voluntary basis and the Parish Council cover the costs of printing. Copies are delivered to every household in the parish in February, May, August and November each year, and the contents include reports from the various village organisations along with articles and features from and about the people, past and present of the parish.

NEWSLETTER No 1
BECKLEY VILLAGE HALL

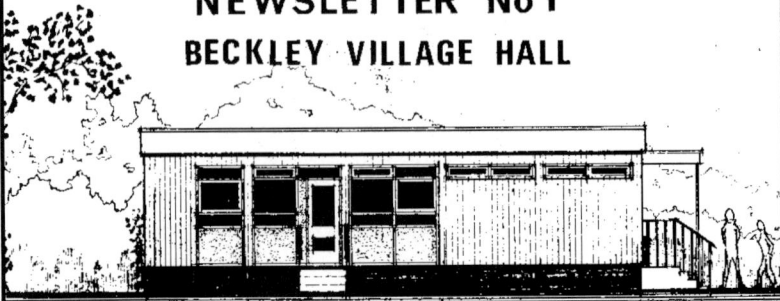

This is the first Village Hall Newsletter and I know very well, it won't be the last you will receive in the next few years!!

* * * * *

We have nearly made it !!! In the last few weeks the new Hall, has really taken shape. All internal partitions have now been erected, plumbing works together with electrical fittings are now being fitted. This last weekend we treated the whole of the external walls with "Chestnut" preservative, which has made a real difference to the Halls appearance.

* * * * *

Recently, we had a visit from Mel Smith, Oxfordshire Rural Community Council. She was really taken-a-back by the shear speed, that the project has progressed and also by the enthusiasm of the construction team.

* * * * *

We have applied to Register the new Village Hall as a Charity, this will not attract rates from the South Oxfordshire District Council, which in turn will help our finances.

* * * * *

Help is still needed to complete the Hall, if you could lend a hand i.e. dig trenches, mix concrete, wheel a wheelbarrow, paint, clean windows or just tidy and sweep up, please come along any Saturday or Sunday morning, between the hours of 10.00 a.m.-1.00 p.m.

* * * * *

The First Village Newsletter.

Chapter Thirteen

The Women's Institute

Beckley Women's Institute was formed in December 1925. Mrs Newell, a founder member, was quoted in the local press in 1966 as saying, "Mrs Holland Hibbert told me she wanted to start an Institute here, and asked me if I would help her. I told her I didn't know anything about Institutes, and she said she didn't either, I thought that was a promising start!"

After being suspended in June 1944 the Institute was

Beckley Women's Institute members circa 1936/37.
In this picture there is unusually a male member, a young John Wing in the arms of his mother.

169

reformed in March 1948 with a record membership of 42. The local press reported in their WI Diary section that "At the June 1948 meeting Beckley WI had a talk on household repairs followed by the distribution of the contents of a large parcel from a WI in Alberta Canada."

Glancing through the records it's noticeable that the change in women's working patterns has affected membership numbers - these were at their peak in the late forties, the fifties and sixties. The special events and courses mirror what was happening both locally, nationally and internationally: raising the money for a village nurse in 1927, wartime cookery and make do and mend courses in the 1940's, raising money for Hungarian relief in 1956 and 57, a questionnaire on the village bus problems in 1975, a tea stall at the village fete to celebrate the royal wedding in 1981. The range of activities has changed from dressmaking and cookery through rug-making and lampshades to making corn dollies and wine. Nowadays we are asking for courses on T'ai Chi Chuan and making the most of..........not only your garden but also the Internet.

Some memories

"We used to meet in the WI room at Grove Cottage which was small and up the steps. There was a sink in the corner, you could boil a kettle. People were packed in but it was a good atmosphere. This however changed with the move to the school hall. We weren't allowed to use the kitchen so we had to take flasks of hot water to make our tea and the fuses used to blow. We began meeting in the village hall in 1982."

"If the WI room was too cold in the late 1970's,

170

Mauveen Pether's dressmaking classes were held in her house. Kate Lea used to come along even though her fingers were all thumbs. It was good fun."

"I do remember that the entertainment at the Christmas parties was all done by members. It was great fun - skits and comic turns were the general rule. We ended up singing carols and Elfrieda Andrews always sang Silent Night in her native German Language. Everybody brought a contribution of something they had cooked for the refreshments."

"In the days when cars and outings weren't so plentiful, WI trips were special events - London bound, members went off to such places as Westminster, The Royal Academy and The Royal Mint. At one time the committee used to organise mystery tours, one of these was a memorable trip by canal long boat along the Oxford Canal stopping for tea at Kidlington."

Since its inauguration in 1926, the following have served as Presidents of the Beckley WI: Mrs Holland Hibbert, Mrs H Newell, Mrs Chaundy, Miss Staveley, Mrs Maxted, Mrs Quartermain, Miss Kennedy, Mrs Andrews, Lady de Villiers, Mrs Tilbury, Mrs Steward, Miss Lea, Mrs Gibson, Mrs Lockhart-Smith, Mrs Soanes, Sue Lankester, Val Roberts, Marion Weinstein and Liz Reis.

Fashions come and go but the main aims of the WI remain the same. Members from years ago would feel at home with the basic plan of the meetings, we still have the same seasonal events and continue to take part in the local Woodperry Group, County and National events, but things have changed! Perhaps not so daringly as in North Yorkshire (with their saucy calendar) but changed they have. However as the retiring President said at an AGM - "We still enjoy meeting, welcoming new people, keeping in touch with everyone and all having, as members, a role to play."

Barbara Wharton.

In 1965 the Beckley WI entered a scrapbook in a Jubilee Competition and came first in Oxfordshire. Subsequently the book was shown in the National Exhibition and in response to many requests was produced in booklet form and entitled "Signpost to Beckley", a portrait of the village in 1965. It has proved to be very popular was reprinted is often quoted from and still sought after. The original can be seen by arrangement with the current President or Secretary.

W.I. Members on a post WW2 outing to Job's Dairy at Didcot.

172

Chapter Fourteen

The School

As early as 1764 there was a charity left by Stephen Wheatfield the Rector of the Parish of Stanton-St-John and his wife Margaret, a yearly sum of about £6 to pay for the education of 10 poor children of Beckley and Horton. In 1819 £3.9s.4d (about £3.46 today) was paid to a schoolmaster in Beckley to educate 6 children in reading and writing and £3 to a schoolmaster in Horton to teach 4 children. There were also 3 endowed schools in the parish for 70 to 120 children, one in Beckley and two in Horton. Bearing in mind that the Parish then covered a very much bigger area and included Horton, Studley, and Whitehorse Green, together with the two long since gone ancient settlements of Marlake and Ash stretching almost to Murcot. The school was situated in what is now part of Grove Cottage. In 1833 the school at Beckley was for 24 boys and 26 girls; 12 children were educated free and 27 paid for by the Rector. In the 1840's the schoolmaster was named Wells who had served in the Peninsular War and was believed to have fought against the French at the Battle of Corunna in 1809. He was later succeeded by James Henry Dickenson.

January 1st 1883, an important date for the school, saw the start of Henry Tossell's engagement as headmaster. He was to continue at the school until September 1922. Five years after his appointment, Government Inspectors, although praising Mr Tossell for improvements to the school nevertheless were complaining that the schoolroom of 80 cubic feet was very crowded and that 'the infants room is so small that no gallery or desks can be introduced '. In 1892 there were 100 children on roll and the inspectors complained that the infants and first standard were being taught in a room measuring 14ft. 3ins. with only one small window for ventilation. In addition all infant's and girl's hats and cloaks were hung on the walls of the room. By May of that year the Government were insisting that the 1st standard should move into the main schoolroom and that ventilation be improved. This was done but there was still no room for desks. In May 1894 the Managers received notice that 'My Lords cannot continue recognition of the existing infant's room beyond the current year ending March 31st. 1895. No grant can be made for any period after that date.' Meanwhile, in 1893 Beckley school with an attendance of 86 was affiliated to the National Society from which a grant of £40 was received towards the provision of a new building.

Pupils of Beckley School in Church Street, probably around the turn of the century. Note the boys all have caps and stiff collars and the girls hats and pinafores.

174

The 'New' School

On January 16th. 1885 the school was closed all day to enable the children to present an entertainment in aid of the Building Fund for erecting a new school. Three months later on April 18th. the Lord Bishop of Oxford laid the Foundation stone of the new building. The next day the children purchased bricks at one (old) penny a time and laid them each side of the stone. I remember farmer Ted Hall's brother Alfred was always keen and proud to point out the position in the wall of the brick he had purchased.

On September 11th. Mr Tossell wrote, "Re-opened today and commenced work in the new school, 88 present. I have explained several rules necessary for the proper assembling of the children." The building consisted of two rooms separated by a wooden screen. The latter was so heavy that it required several strong men to move it. There were two small cloakrooms for the boys and girls entered from their separate playgrounds. The outside toilets were across the playgrounds.

Schools during this time were much more affected by children's health and parents' work than in modern days. Several times the school was closed owing to illness. In 1890 influenza caused a weeks closure and in 1906 the master complains that he had one of the most dreadful weeks he had ever experienced in any school. Severe colds and violent coughs meant that "ordinary lessons were quite out of the question. I have tried to combat it with drill and singing lessons." Later that year the school was closed from September 26th. until November 13th. because of whooping cough. Even then attendances were low until the Christmas holiday. Even those who escaped the illnesses had days off to fetch medicines from Wheatley or Islip. In 1902 a visiting inspector wrote in his report, "The infant room is very cold. A thermometer should be provided. I note also that no sponge or water is provided for cleaning slates - spitting is both dirty and likely to carry infection - sore throats exist."

The weather also affected schooling. Mr Tossell notes absences caused by violent storms, snow, torrential rains, intense heat, and wet fields (pupils unable to walk across to school). Another reason for absence was working in the fields. Children went haymaking, potato gathering, shooting and woodcarrying. In September 1902 half of the children were absent due to the late harvest and the corn being so beaten down that more fagging had to be done than for several years past. As so many children were out in the hayfields the Managers decided to close the school.

During the period of Mr Tossell's headship it was the practice to employ young people who had not long finished normal schooling, as pupil/teachers. Two that are known are Alfred Hall around the turn of the century and Esme Wheeler in the early 1920's.

The End of an Era

September 29th 1922 saw Mr Tossell's retirement as Headmaster on October 6th. he was presented with a clock and a cheque at a large gathering when many expressed their gratitude for his 'unflagging services' to the school and village.

In 1924 attendance at the school fell to 30 when pupils over 11 years of age were transferred for secondary education to Stanton-St-John, staying until they were 14 and travelling there on bicycles provided free of charge.

My personal memories of the school in the early 1930's

are of Headmistress Rosie Higgs sitting at her high desk, rapping the cane on the desk top and pursing her lips when she was annoyed. Rosie was appointed as monitress at the school in 1913 and later became headmistress. At one time I cut my knee badly to which Rosie rendered first aid, in the process her white blouse being well covered by my blood.

The facilities at the school at that time were not very adequate by today's standards, although accepted as normal for the time. Heating was by means of two large cast iron stoves one in each room. When stoked up the stoves glowed red and fire guard rails were necessary to avoid accidental burns. Needless to say the heating wasn't very efficient, a similar situation occurring to that in the church whereby you roasted in front but froze at the back. When the wind was strong in a certain direction the smoke often blew back down

Upper standard class of 1901 with headmaster Mr Tossell and Mrs Tossell who taught needlework. Pupil teacher Alf Hall is extreme right.

177

the chimney into the room. The outside toilets were cold and damp in the winter and in the summer the smell was almost unbearable! Not a place to linger for very long at any season

A Beckley School picture taken around 1926, dress is less formal at this time. Teachers Miss Kyte and Miss Phillips.

of the year. When I left I went to Oxford to school and for a long time felt annoyed that I had missed out on the free bike given to those who went on to Stanton.

The next ten years included the period of the Second World War when a number of children evacuated from East London attended the school. No war damage was suffered by the school building, but it was an unsettling and turbulent time when no one knew what the future would bring, hardly an environment conducive to good learning. No new building work could be carried out to improve the facilities available, and repairs were largely just 'patching up and making do'. Shortages of most things made life very difficult and which hardly improved for some time after the cessation of hostilities.

After the War ended, a population explosion and expectations of better standards of accommodation and education put the school system under severe pressure and there was great discussion (and rumours abounded) about closures and amalgamations of schools, all much too tedious to be recorded here. There was an examination taken at 11 years of age and called the 'Eleven-plus,' the results of which decided where pupils would go for their secondary education. Boys from Beckley School who passed the examination went on to Lord Williams Grammar School at Thame and the girls to Wheatley Park, the other children went to Wheatley Secondary Modern. Eventually this divisive examination was abandoned and all the secondary schools became comprehensive with no segregation of sexes and equal opportunities for all.

Changes for the Better   By John Amor

By the summer of 1961 the number of children at the school had increased so much that plans were made to teach one class in the village playing field pavilion. However, as parents objected to this plan it was decided that children from Horton-cum-Studley should transfer to Sandhills School. Consequently, when I took over as head from Molly Lewis in September there were only 33 children on roll from the villages of Beckley and Elsfield. However, numbers rose over the next few years. Already by early 1962 several Horton parents were asking to send their children to Beckley and by 1965 sixteen of the 57 children on roll came from Horton-cum-Studley. At this time the staff consisted of the head and Mrs Benson, the Vicars wife who taught the infants.

At the end of my first term we experienced the coldest Christmas of recent times. Water pipes in the school froze and when they burst water flooded both classrooms. In addition the cisterns in the outside toilets froze, a problem that was repeated in 1963 when they were frozen from January until March. As a result, the toilet cubicles were roofed over and electric heaters installed. Other improvements in the first few years included new lighting, and the sanding and sealing of floors in the classrooms, provision of a large climbing frame and a swimming pool.

The 1930's, most of the pupils can be identified by our older residents. The Headmistress, Miss Rosie Higgs is on the extreme right.

In my first year, the County Council had plans for a new school to be built in the Woodperry Road. When this idea was abandoned, the site in Church Street was expanded, taking in the adjoining orchard and land to the south of the school, with a widened vehicle entrance and a separate footpath pedestrian entrance for the children. A piece of 'Home Close' field was also acquired for games pitches.

Numbers continued to grow and a part-time teacher was appointed. A music teacher came every Friday afternoon and a remedial teacher also visited the school twice a week and taught a group of children in the cloakroom, which she shared with the newly appointed school secretary and classroom assistant Mrs Winfield. This of course, was not a satisfactory situation, and was reminiscent of the 1894 infant room when children were taught with hats and coats hung around the room! The cloakroom was also used by the school doctor, the speech therapist, the dentist and children doing remedial foot exercises with the visiting P.E. expert. If a parent or visitor wished to talk to the head privately the cloakroom was the only place available. When the telephone was installed in 1964 the cloakroom once again came into its own. On one occasion, however, Mrs Benson answering the phone spent rather more time than she expected in the cloakroom when the door jammed and could not be opened for some time!

The number of children continued to increase and in 1968 a new two-class infant room was built on the other side of the playground. Building started on February 26th. and completion was expected in eight weeks time. However when the brickwork was at window top height it was condemned and taken down and rebuilt. This resulted in a shortage of bricks causing delays. Many problems arose and more walls were again rebuilt. Finally the building was complete although the inside walls were deemed to be sub-standard. It had taken seven months to complete the building. The Victorians took four months back in 1895!

With the new building completed, the children were divided into three classes. Mrs Benson and newly appointed Mrs Alcock taught classes in the new building whilst I continued to teach the upper juniors in the old building. In 1969 with the number on roll over 80, a part-time teacher joined the staff. By May 1971 the number was 94 with children coming from Beckley, Horton-cum-Studley, Elsfield, the Bayswater Road, Woodperry, Murcott and Fencott. Children from Horton were brought by bus and those from Elsfield by mini-bus. To enable children to visit Oxford and other villages for football and netball matches the school joined with Stanton St John and purchased an old ambulance which was then converted into a mini-bus. Another development was the formation of 'The Friends of Beckley School'. Since that time 'The Friends' have purchased many items for the school, replaced the swimming pool with a permanent one and arranged for its heating.

In February 1974 another classroom was added to the school, together with a staff room, heads room and toilets. Also in 1974 the old cloakroom and scullery were demolished and replaced by a large kitchen so we were able to have our own cook to provide school meals rather than having them supplied from Sandhills canteen. With the new classrooms, the juniors moved out of the Victorian building which became the school hall and was used for assemblies, P.E. (a climbing frame had been installed), music ,drama, concerts and a dining hall.

The new junior room consisted of a general teaching area, an art/craft area and a well stocked library used by all the school. This was later extended when the lower juniors moved into a mobile classroom in 1988. In 1977 three ex-pupils painted the school mini-bus with the popular Muppet characters and the vehicle was henceforth known as the Muppet-van. Later the van was replaced by a modern purpose-built mini-bus.

Playlink, a pre-school scheme was started in 1975 and continued every Tuesday afternoon. This enabled children to get to know the school before starting in the infant class and was found to be very beneficial. From 1971 regular school newsletters were given to all parents and later a school brochure was produced. In October 1981 the school appeared on television. A national company were making a film about Mother Frances and her appeal for the Helen House Hospice. Mother Frances asked for part of the film to be made at Beckley School as she found the children so responsive at an earlier visit. The filming took place during the half-term holiday and was broadcast later in the Autumn.

In the 1960's the parents were very much against school uniforms but twenty years later a blue sweatshirt with a Beckley motif was introduced at the suggestion of the parents. The wearing of this was optional but it became very popular and most children were pleased to wear it to school.

The Federation and Beyond

January 1982 saw significant changes take place in the school. Owing to a fall in the numbers in both Beckley and Stanton St John schools, the two schools were federated with myself as the head of both. Stanton juniors were moved to Beckley whilst the infants continued to be taught at both schools. The combined school served five parishes with 94 children on roll.

Two years later the County Council decided to close both schools and open a new school on both sites. With so few children at Stanton, this enabled them in July 1984 to close the Stanton site without going through the normal procedure for closing a school. At the same time internal changes were made to the Beckley buildings to form three classrooms.

The school is a Church of England School and each morning began with an assembly. The children regularly took part, reading, acting, singing and playing their instruments. After the Federation, both the Revd de Vere and the Revd Michael Farthing, took assemblies on Friday mornings and also took groups with the help of Miss Lea, a churchwarden of Beckley and a friend of the school. Miss Lea used to comment that she was most impressed by the confidence and friendliness of the children. A visiting remedial teacher once remarked "It was the happiest school I have ever been in."

At the end of the 1989 summer term I retired after 28 years as head of Beckley School. As a complete surprise I was collected from my home by helicopter and with Mrs Amor was flown to Beckley where we landed on the school playing field. At the school about 250 people awaited our arrival and after speeches watched my second surprise of the evening when most of the May Queens of the last twenty seven years came forward to greet me on the platform. Gemma Dingle on behalf of the school, past and present, presented 'Sir' with a computer and the Friends of Beckley School gave a specially painted watercolour of the view from the school field.

John Amor

On the 3rd of May 1995 the centenary of the old building was marked by the unveiling of a Commemoration Stone by the Bishop of Oxford, the Rt. Rev Richard Harries. The stone is situated alongside the original Foundation stone. The ceremony was attended by pupils, past and present, parents, teachers and staff, and former dinner ladies. This was followed by another 'get together' of old pupils and John Amor staged an exhibition of school photographs and memorabilia.

Now at the turn of the century and millennium, the school continues to prosper under Headteacher Mrs Grace Zawadski who succeeded Richard Foulkes in 1993.

'From Little Acorns do mighty Oak trees grow' - The Playgroup

Beckley Playgroup was started in 1976 by Jan Weller in her house in Otmoor Lane. It consisted of three children, Richard Weller, Martha Lane-Fox and Harriet Lockhart-Smith. From then on pressure brought on by additional numbers meant a move to Manor House which was also soon outgrown. The next move was to High Corner House where Rosemary Tulloch had a spare playroom. Because of the lack of playgroup facilities in the neighbouring villages numbers still kept rising and the situation became desperate. Rose Fernie from Grove House suggested the old WI room, but there were no toilet facilities. The fathers then set to work digging the drains and fitting the toilet which was a great 'relief' for the problem of needing more space.

Then in 1982, due to the merging of Beckley and Stanton Schools, a room became vacant at Stanton with central heating and a cheap rent. It was at this time that the parents decided as a tribute and thanks for the work put in by Jan, to rename the group 'The Jan Weller Playgroup'.

Five village elders, 1970.
All one time pupils of Beckley School.
Left to right :- Harry Newell, Harold Lambourne, Arthur Payne, Henry Wakelin, Alf Sumner.

Reproduced by courtesy of The Oxford Times.

Chapter Fifteen

Old Village Families

The Wings, the Shop and the Post Office:
A Debt to Dr. Pink   by John Wing

In his novel Cripps the Carrier Richard Doddridge
Blackmore said that the Beckley carrier's fourth son,
Numbers, was to be the butcher of Beckley and his fifth son,
Deuteronomy, its shoemaker. Fact, however, is stranger than
fiction for in that same year, 1877, a poor boy from Stanton St
John crossed the parish boundary into Beckley to learn that
trade which was to have been Deuteronomy's.

Born into a farm labourer's family living in a rented
cottage, no longer extant, at the bottom of Woodperry Hill,
Henry Wing had the good fortune, at the age of 14, to serve an
apprenticeship under James Field, shoemaker and brother of
John Field, landlord of the Abingdon Arms. The
apprenticeship was arranged in consideration of £20 by the
Trustees of Dr. Pink's Charity who paid £10 on the 13th of
January 1877 and the balance of £10 on the 1st January 1880.
(Dr. Robert Pink, Warden of New College, Oxford and Rector
of Stanton St John, had bequeathed £110 in 1647 for
apprenticing children of the parish to tradesmen outside the

parish.)

After serving his seven year apprenticeship Henry married Mary Webb of Stoke Talmage on the 16th June 1884 and rented from the Cooke family part of what is now St Mary's Cottage. While there Henry continued his shoemaking and mending and he and Mary raised three sons, Henry, William and Amos, and two daughters, Annie and Catherine (Kit).

By the turn of the century New Ridge in Church Street had ceased to be an orphanage for girls and the Cooke family kindly allowed the Wings to rent it in lieu of St Mary's Cottage. Henry made and mended shoes in what was formerly the

Henry, Kit and Amos Wing

matron's room and he set up a shop and Post Office in the room by the front door. The sub-postmaster was expected to be in attendance from 8.00am-8.00pm on weekdays and from 8.00am-10.00am and 12.45pm-1.00pm on Sundays. His salary was based on the unit amount of business transacted and not on the number of hours worked except that an hour worked on a Sunday counted as 1200 units.

The Pensions Act of 1908 authorised the Post Office to start paying Old Age Pensions, 5s.0d. (25p) a week each for the over 70's irrespective of sex. In its first full year of operation 832 orders (£208) were paid to 16 pensioners bringing an additional £1.14s. 0d. (£1.70p) to the sub-postmaster's salary. As can be seen from the high number of postal orders issued and cashed, the Post Office acted as the village bank. Similarly the large number of telegrams handled meant that it was the communications' centre not only for Beckley but also for Elsfield, Horton-cum-Studley and Noke. The delivery of telegrams to Noke was particularly bad as it meant walking across fields in all weathers. On 27th October 1909 Henry Wing wrote to the Postmaster at Oxford asking if the telegrams for Noke could be delivered by road from Islip as he had to walk through a wood and flooded fields "which is a very bad journey on dark nights". The Postmaster replied in typical bureaucratic fashion on the 1st November "Your office is nearer than Islip and additional expense would be incurred in delivering from Islip...there appears to be no reason for departing from the general rule". By the start of the First World War Henry's annual salary had increased to £32.13s.0d. (£32.65p) and he had in addition the net profits from the shoe business and the shop.

On the 10th November 1915 Capt. W Owen, the Recruiting Officer at Cowley Barracks, sent to all Post Offices in Oxfordshire railway warrants to be given to any man wishing to enlist in the army at 5s.0d (25p) a day. Tempted no doubt by the railway warrant Amos enlisted in the Devonshire Regiment in preference to the Oxfordshire and Buckinghamshire Light Infantry which many of his friends had joined never to return. His brother William became a Sapper in the Royal Engineers while Henry the eldest brother worked on the railway in Derby and was exempt from military service. With his sons away from home Henry Wing had to rely on his wife and daughters to assist in the shop and Post Office. They must have done remarkably well as Amos was employed at the Post Office in Oxford and Wheatley on his demobilisation.

After the war came two great events in the history of Beckley, the sale of the Bertie Estate in 1919 and part of the Cooke Estate in 1921. New Ridge was included in the latter and was bought by Michael Soanes of Stanton St John. He continued to let it to the Wings until the death of Henry on 19th April 1925 when Amos took over the shop and Post Office and bought New Ridge for £350. With Henry's death the shoemaking and mending ceased. The tools of his trade can be seen at Combe Mill on its open days.

On the 17th September 1926 there was further sadness in the Wing household when Henry's widow Mary died leaving Amos and Kit to run the business, Annie having married and emigrated to New Zealand. This must have been a hectic time for both of them as Amos not only had to be on duty in the Post Office from 6.50am to 7.15pm on weekdays and 9.00am to 10.30am on Sundays and Bank Holidays but he played the violin at local dances on Saturday evenings and as a church warden faithfully attended church every Sunday. His violin playing ceased, however, when on the 29th December 1929 he rolled his Singer Junior motor car on the Common Road and damaged the tendons in his right hand.

Meanwhile when John Clare sold the Manor Farm Estate in 1927 Amos had bought the barns (now Stoneycroft) for £220 with a view to having the shop and Post Office in the centre of the village. He had the ground floor converted by Hector Wheeler which he then let temporarily to a Mr Pownall. He decided against converting the room nearest the road into a shop and instead had a double fronted shop specially built by Mr Wheeler in 1933. On Boxing Day the same year he married Rhoda Charlett and they moved into the new premises soon afterwards. Kit moved with them and New Ridge was let.

During the Second World War the Wings had the arduous task of coping with rationing which continued until Christmas 1953 and Amos had the additional responsibility of being in charge of the Air Raid Precautions Wardens.

The Post Office was busy too. At the start of the war the Chancellor of the Exchequer launched a national savings campaign which became 'War

Amos Wing

Weapons Week' in 1941, 'Warships Week' in 1942, 'Wings for Victory' in 1943 and 'Salute the Soldier' in 1944. During the 'Wings for Victory' week Beckley raised the large sum of £1421.6s.2d. (£1421.31p.) way above its target of £500. From the 13th-20th October 1945 there was a special thanksgiving week in which Beckley raised £830.

Throughout the war Amos managed on a meagre petrol ration to run his Vauxhall 10 to Oxford to collect essential supplies and he continued to sell limited quantities of paraffin under licence from the Petroleum Board. In addition licences were required to sell patent medicines and tobacco. Of the former cough mixtures called 'Kilkof' and 'Newkler' come to mind and of the latter 'Coachman', 'A1', 'Tom Long', 'Old Holborn', 'St Julien', 'Juggler', 'Digger Honey Dew', 'Black Beauty' and 'Black Bell'. From 1949 Pensioners who smoked were issued with a book of tokens each worth 2s.4d. (11p) to be used weekly in the purchase of tobacco. Amos's brother Henry took advantage of this State generosity only to die of cancer in 1966. How public and political opinion has changed in 50 years!

In 1949 Amos's wife Rhoda achieved immortal fame in a book on Oxfordshire in Paul Elek's *'Vision of England'* series. The author Reginald Turnor, said "The map makes much of a Roman Villa at Beckley and, never having seen this, I went into a little village shop and asked the excellent woman behind a tenebrous counter where the villa was and if there was much to be seen there. She said she thought very little, and directed me to a farm down the hill. Then she called to her good man in the parlour behind the shop: "Is there anything left of the Roman villa, Amos?" It was delightful - one of those sayings, phrasings, timings, which come so rarely to charm the explorer." Although the shop sold most things it did not sell Roman artefacts.

Amos's salary as sub-postmaster in 1950 was £130 with an additional allowance of £4.5s.0d. (£4.25p.) for having a public telephone call box in the passage behind the shop. In the same year the net profit from the shop was £209. On the 16th April 1950 the Post Office closed for the first time on a Sunday. Telegram deliveries from Beckley ceased on the 28th

September 1953. The number of telegrams received had peaked with 1394 in 1910 by 1950, due to the increasing number of telephone subscribers, the number had fallen to 258. The forwarding of telegrams from Beckley ceased on 31st December 1959.

During the winters of 1947 and 1963, when Beckley was cut off by snow for several days, the shop was the village lifeline but regrettably at 10am on the 6th July 1963 the shop and Post Office closed due to Amos's ill-health. He died four months later. His sons had no desire to carry on the business. In the previous year John had been appointed Assistant Librarian at Christ Church, Oxford where he was to remain until retirement, and David was a student at University College London. The net profit when the shop closed was the same as it was 13 years earlier but the Post Office salary had risen to £288.17s.6d. (£288.87½p) although it was to have

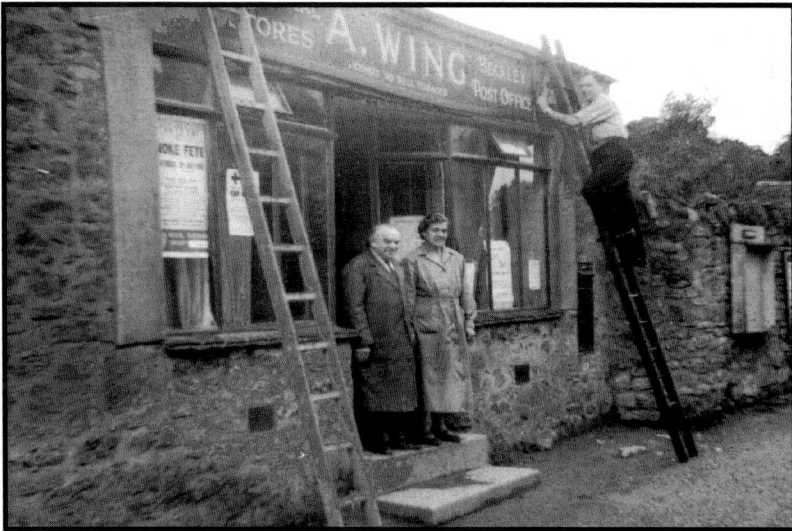

The shop closes, Amos, Rhoda and John Wing.

been reduced by £36 in 1964 due to a decline in some classes of business. In the same year the Resale Prices Act came into force. By abolishing resale price maintenance this act was the death knell for village shops giving the green light to the supermarkets which could sell goods cheaper than the village shops could buy them. Following the closure the Oxford Post Office ran a restricted service from 9.30am to noon every Thursday in the old WI room for paying pensions and selling stamps and postal orders. Notwithstanding the forebodings on its viability Mrs Holland-Hibbert sold 'Binfield' to Michael Sumner on condition he opened a shop and Post Office there. He in turn sold it to John Howse but it was clearly unviable and closed after a few years to become a family home called 'Crowshott' (now 'Rhulen').

With this decline of the village shop, in 1977 the enterprising Tim Gresswell started a mobile bus shop visiting Oxfordshire villages twice a week. At first the bus was a single decker, then a double decker and eventually an articulated vehicle called the 'Road Market'. Mr Gresswell sold the business to Michael and Christina Woodward in the mid-1980's. They ran it for a few years until the cost of maintaining the vehicle and the competition from the supermarkets proved prohibitive. The vehicle now languishes on Otmoor Park. In addition Beckley has had a variety of itinerant salesmen over the years offering everything from pots and pans to wet fish. It is an appropriate end to this century that we find there at the Royal Oak Farm the only shop in the parish run by Michael Soanes and family whose homonymous ancestor once owned the house in Beckley in which the Wings first set up the shop and Post Office a hundred years ago.

John Wing. 1999

The Cookes

The Cooke family have roots in many parts of the country and many male offspring through the ages were ordained into the Church. There was a strong literary tendency in the family with several of them becoming very famous writers and enjoyed the friendship of well known others in the same profession. Although over the years there were connections with Oxford, the first mention of Beckley was when a Samuel Cooke married Cassandra Leigh, second daughter of Dr. Leigh, Master of Balliol and Miss Bee of Beckley. They went to live at Great Bookham, Surrey where Samuel was Vicar for fifty two years, Cassandra did not enjoy very good health and bore several children who died with only three surviving Theophilus, George and Mary.

Theophilus remained a bachelor and went to live at Beckley in Grove House which he had inherited from his grandmother (Bee). He became perpetual curate of Beckley Parish which was then very much larger and included Horton and Studley. He had a reputation for being a rather 'lively gentleman,' he entertained a lot and it was said that at his grand dinner parties "no one but titled ladies sat down". He would ride often to Oxford and back and there is a story that his ghost still haunts the Grove, he has been seen at night riding his grey horse down the drive and into the stable. A cousin of Theophilus was Jane Austen the novelist who refers to the family in her letters which were published by Oxford University Press. Theophilus' brother George who was vicar of Cubbington in Warwickshire, married Anne Hay the daughter of a London merchant. They had six children Helen, Samuel, Caroline, George, Julia and William. Samuel was educated at Rugby, Charterhouse and Christ Church, he was ordained and held the livings at Benson and Great Budworth in Cheshire, the latter being a Christ Church living. He married Nina Clowes and as he suffered from asthma he took the living at Northbourne in Kent hoping to derive benefit from the East coast climate. There were six children, five born at Budworth and the youngest at Northbourne. Samuel died in 1877 at Northbourne and his widow and children came to live in Oxford.

The second son, George Theophilus went to Rugby and Corpus Christi, and became a fellow of Magdalen. He became his uncles curate at Beckley and interested himself very much in Horton and did much good work there. After the death of his uncle in 1846 he became vicar of Beckley, which was then separated as a parish from Horton. His mother and sisters came to live with him at the Grove. Between them they built a church, school and a vicarage at Horton and installed the first incumbent the Rev. P Hutchinson.

The family in Beckley seemed to be very comfortably off keeping many servants; butler, lady's maid, coachman, gardener and so on ... Mrs Cooke was apparently a very attractive old lady but very much under the thumb of her second daughter Caroline who was much given to good works and founded a orphanage for boys at Cubbington, she later brought them to Beckley putting them in the house called Oldridge (now called Grove Farmhouse). She also founded a girl's orphanage after building a house to accommodate them in Church Street which was called 'Newridge'. The house was for some time the village Post Office and Shop. Caroline was very much the strong character of the family, deeply religious and autocratic, ran the parish, the school, the choir, the girl's and the boy's orphanages, and according to John

Ruskin a friend of the family, also ran the farm very well. Arthur Cooke told of his mother remembering Caroline at church services sitting behind her orphans and prodding them if they misbehaved. Old residents often told a story that after Sunday service absentee churchgoers would receive a visit from Caroline to enquire the reason for non-attendance, when the excuse was because of illness she would produce a bottle of 'physic' (castor oil?) to administer to the sufferer, it is not known how she treated the parishioners who were absent for other reasons, probably gave them a double dose! After Mrs Cooke's death Julia moved away and Caroline and George continued to live in Beckley until 1894 when he unfortunately took carbolic acid by mistake and died. Caroline then went to live in Oxford and Samuel's widow Nina moved from there to Beckley. The Grove had belonged to her since her husbands death but she had stayed in Oxford for the sake of the children's education. She was always very anxious that a vicarage be provided in Beckley and foresaw difficulties in accommodating future incumbents. It is thought that she was responsible for the building of Grove Farmhouse (now Nokewood House) possibly as a dower house but in such a style that one day it could be used as a vicarage, it was lived in by the Rev. Doyne who succeeded George Theophilus as vicar. The building became the farmhouse in 1916 and was in the tenancy of Edward Hall until the 1960's when it was let as a dwelling.

On Nina's death her sons Samuel and George Cooke continued to live in The Grove until following Samuel's' death in 1921 the house was sold together with other properties of the Grove estates. George then moved in to Grove Farmhouse with the Hall's until his death in 1926.   Alf Senior said of him: "He was always a perfect gentleman - even when he

Samuel and George Cooke.

was drunk he was a perfect gentleman."

    Samuel and George's brother William married Hilda Mace and they had eight children. William was a curate in Birmingham, vicar of Horton-cum Studley and towards the end of his life vicar of Yarnton. After his death Hilda lived in Rawlinson Road and later Lathbury Road in Oxford, before moving in the 1950's to Manor Farmhouse Beckley. She was a marvellous lady always with a kind word to all she met or visited. She would walk in the village, ramrod straight dressed in a long black dress buttoned to the neck and a severe broad rimmed black hat placed squarely on her head. She died in 1973 in her 101st year. Two of her children, Hilda and Nina lived at some time in Beckley either at Manor Farmhouse or Nokewood House. Her second son William Arthur was born at Horton-cum Studley, educated at King Edward's School Birmingham and briefly at St Chad's Theological College, Durham. In 1979 he came to live in Beckley with his wife Pam to the renovated Otmoor Cottage, in Church Street.

198

Sadly, in 1985 Pam died and subsequently Arthur (as he was better known in Beckley) sold the cottage and moved to Nokewood House. Until his death in July 1999 he was for several years Beckley's oldest inhabitant. He has a daughter Patricia who lives in the United States and a son Robert living in Kent.

Details for the above kindly provided by Robert Cooke and Ellinor Nina Gardner the grand-daughter of the late Nina Mary Beachcroft née Cooke.

The Holland-Hibbert's and Grove House.

A reminiscence by Michael Holland -Hibbert. (Now The Viscount Knutsford.)

My parents, Wilfred and Audrey Holland-Hibbert, bought Grove House with 30 acres in 1925 and moved in with my two sisters Lavinia and Delia, aged 6 and 4 and I was born there in 1926. The house had belonged to an old alcoholic bachelor, George Cooke. It had originally been the rectory and the owners were "Squarsons" who owned about 500 acres around Beckley, including Grove Farm, let to Edward Hall.

Soon after he moved in, my Father was looking around Cookes Copse and nearly caught his leg in a villainous iron man-trap set in the

199

undergrowth to trap poachers. He carefully removed it and hung it on the wall of the stables as a precautionary reminder of the fate which befell trespassers!

My mother designed and completely made the garden which suffered from poor, very dry sandy soil: nevertheless she persisted and with a good eye for planting and colour, she produced a pretty and prolific garden, much admired by visitors when the garden was opened under the National Gardens Scheme. My mother was helped immeasurably by two devoted experienced gardeners, Hubert Atkins and John Wright, who spanned the 52 years that my parents lived in Grove House. In 1977, my mother, by then a widow for 15 years, moved into the Manor Farmhouse, where at the age of 83, she designed and made another small garden which gave her an enjoyable occupation until she died in 1987.

Until the War in 1939, my parents employed indoors a married butler and cook, a Nanny, a 'Tweenie' (between Kitchen and Nursery) and a housemaid. She was Rhoda, later to marry Amos Wing the Postmaster. Rhoda was a very warm-hearted lovely lady who always gave me a smiling welcome and more acceptable, an extra tangerine ball or treacle toffee when I went into the shop to buy 6d (2½ p) worth of sweets. Once I heard that it was the birthday of my elderly grandfather, Lord Knutsford so I bought from Rhoda a 6d (2½p) postal order, instead of sweets and sent it to him as a present.

Hunting and riding played a large part in our family lives. Four hunters were kept with two ponies for my sisters, and they all hunted with the South Oxfordshire Hunt (now the Vale of Aylesbury) or the Bicester. I never liked riding so was excluded! George Newman was our groom for over 30 years, a very nice quiet man with a permanent sniff and devoted to his horses, and uncomplaining about the morning rides to the meets, sometimes up to 12 miles, and the long rides home on tired horses in the dark. In those days motor horse boxes were seldom seen and if a meet with the Bicester Hunt was too far to ride to, the horses were loaded in a horsebox on the train from Islip and returned the same way.

George Newman also looked after our two cars - both Wolseley's. Petrol was delivered weekly in red two gallon cans by a Shell lorry (price 1/6d - 7½p) to fuel the cars and the electricity generator. Each morning George filled up the cars' tanks, cleaned the windscreens and started the engines so they were warm before they were used. But no heat inside of course, only fur or woollen rugs!

In 1926 my mother started the Beckley Women's Institute in a room up very narrow stairs adjacent to the stables and behind the Newman's cottage. They made jam, were taught cookery and cake-making, had travel talks and other useful things. Few if any, of the members owned cars, so the WI was a godsend to them. In addition to the village shop and Post Office ably managed by Amos and Rhoda Wing, there was a village carrier Mr Willis who drove into Oxford three days a week in a cart with an old chestnut horse. He would shop for the whole village from joints of meat to pins and cotton reels.

When the War started in 1939 we queued in the WI room for gas masks, and then about thirty evacuee children arrived from the East End of London. Pat and Grace came to live with us for several years and went to school in Beckley.

They were so unalike that we suspected they were not sisters, Their mother who stayed only one night quickly returning to London, mumbling that the country was much too quiet!

My father commanded a company of the Home Guard which included the Beckley Section led by Sgt Lethbridge assisted by Cpls Hubert Atkins our gardener and Harry Smith our odd-job man. Dressed in khaki battledress, forage caps and long great coats in winter (which they kept and wore long after the war was over), they paraded, exercised and cleaned their scarce and aged weapons every week. They placed a tree trunk in the road near our drive entrance gate so that when the German tanks churned down the hill to destroy our village, they would be stopped in convoy to allow time for the Home Guards to lob home-made petrol bombs over our garden wall on to the tanks and set them on fire. I helped to fill the bottles with petrol then cork them with a fuse sticking through, so I could imagine how effective they would have been if the German tanks had ever arrived !

I well remember the village baker in Church Street watching him shovelling the bread in and out of the oven - dogs, cats and kids everywhere - very good bread but it would not conform with the health regulations of today!

I spent the first twenty years of my life in Beckley. Life was fun and happy because young and old worked and played together and were content to stay in the village, providing their own entertainment which admittedly they were forced to do, because there was only one bus in and out of Oxford on three days a week. But it provided for a happy and friendly atmosphere of which I have many fond memories.

Knutsford

There were two families of Pay(i)ne's in Beckley, not, so far as is known related in any way, as there were also two families of Lambourne's and two of Hall's and three of Sumner's. All very confusing when trying to trace the lineage from the parish records, and to make matters worse they often seemed to give their offspring the same or similar Christian names!

The Payne's and Beckley   by Roger Payne

It was sometime between 1830 and 1834, that Thomas Pay(i)ne and his wife Martha took up residence in Beckley. Their first two children were born in Sandhills, and Beckley was, for what ever reason, where the family settled in the early 1830's in the cottage at the bottom of Church Street, and where they stayed for well over a hundred years, and perhaps would be still were it not for my grandfather.

He was born in Beckley in 1884, the second son of the eight children of Charles Payne. When he left school he went to work in the engine sheds of the Great Western Railway where he began as an 'engine cleaners lad' in 1887, finally settling in Acton in London in the 1920's, having achieved his ambition to become a locomotive engine driver.

Roger Payne

203

The Payne family moved to a cottage further up Church Street and following 'Grandpa' Payne's death, to the cottage at church corner which was half of what is now High Corner House. The last members of the family to live in the cottage were brother and sister Bill and Martha (Rogers' great uncle and aunt). Martha outlived her brother and then resided in one of the bungalows in Roman Way until she too died.

Philip Payne 1932

Descendants of the other Payne family who were market gardeners still live in the village. Mrs Alice Payne, the last to carry the family name died in 1998 at the age of 93, but her daughter Mary Girdler lives with her husband at 'Sandy Acre' Woodperry Road and their son Mark lives in the old family home 'The Bank'. They belong to one of the oldest Beckley families, being able to trace their ancestry back to the early 1700's.

The Hall Families

The Hall family line can also be traced back to the 18th century when forebears came from Stow-on-the-Wold (then on the other side of the world) to farm in Beckley and Oddington. Early movements are obscure, but Tredwell Hall his son Edward Pinniger and then his son Edward George Tredwell were tenant farmers at Lower Park Farm (Beckley

Ted Hall and his nephew Alf Senior

Park) and Lower Farm during the 19th century. The family
lived at one time at 'The Rosary' High Street and Edward
George Tredwell Hall was landlord of the Abingdon Arms in
the early part of the 20th century, he then was tenant at Grove
Farm until shortly before his death in 1966 at the age of ninety
years.

The other family Hall came to the village in 1928 from
the North East of England. Thomas set up a thriving market
garden in Woodperry Road, was a prominent member of the
Parish Council and the Methodist Chapel. His two daughters
Primrose and Joan still live in the village and his son Malcolm
lives in the family home and works the market garden with his
son Kevin.

The Sumner Families

Of the Sumner families, there are several still living in the village. Malcolm who lives at 'Sandy Warren' New Inn Road is the only one left of that particular family who first came to live in Church Street and then to Rose Cottage in High Street. Another Sumner family came to Beckley at the end of the18th century living in what is now called 'Gordons Cottage' in Otmoor Lane. Several of the descendants were born and married in Beckley. Jan Weller is a member of this

Mary Sumner outside 'Gordon's Cottage'

family and lives in Otmoor Lane although not in the old family home. The third family of Sumner's also lived in Otmoor Lane, Tom Sumner's widow Grace still lives there in the family home. It is thought the three families are not related other than being distant cousins. A family of Sumner's were supposedly living in Beckley in the reign of Elizabeth the First and it is most likely that it is Tom's ancestors that go back that far.

There are obviously more families who might have been mentioned such as Clarke, Gatz, Hayden, Hudson, Lambourne, Newell, Shipley, Soanes, Wakelin and Williams, and others known to me, but having omitted to obtain information when the old inhabitants were still alive, I must apologise for being unable to write more fully about them, you will however, find many of the names referred to or individual family members written about under other headings elsewhere in the book.

An outing from the Methodist Chapel before the Second World war in which many old Beckley families are represented.

Harry Newman and Hector Wheeler on the steps of Amos Wing's new shop in the High Street. 1933.

Chapter Sixteen

Memories

This chapter consists of a collection of individual memories of the village and its environs. The first by Harry Newell, an old Beckley stalwart who served as a Special Constable for many years rising to the rank of Inspector.

Personal Memories   by Harry L. Newell

My memory takes me back to the day when I was first allowed to attend the Beckley Church of England School. I was then three and a half years of age - the year 1904. Reading, writing and arithmetic seemed to be the only subjects taught. Each morning school started with a short service of about 15 minutes in the Church. We then marched back to school when the vicar took the higher standards in Religious Knowledge until 10.00am. There were two rooms in the school - the big room and the infant room. Mr Tossell was Headmaster and taught standards 1 to 6 in the big room. Standard 6 was the highest that could be reached. After reaching standard 6, I spent quite a lot of time checking the lower standard's work and writing out notices for the Oddfellows Club of which Mr Tossell was secretary. During the haymaking season my mother obtained permission from Mr Tossell for me to leave school at 3.30 pm to take tea to my father in the fields. The normal time for school to close was 4.00 pm. Children left school at the age of 13 years. I have no recollection of anyone being punished in school. Each Sunday from the age of 4 years, I attended Sunday school at 10.00am, Morning Service at 11.00am and children's service at 3.00pm. After the age of 6 years I was allowed to join the choir and go to Evening Service. On Easter Sunday morning and on Christmas morning the choir boys went to the vicarage for breakfast, a custom that was dropped after 1915. There was always a full congregation at morning and evening services, men predominated in the mornings and women in the evenings. The church was always packed to capacity on Easter Day and especially at Harvest Festival.

Another of my early memories was of the church bell ringers practising on Tuesday and Thursday evenings after the 5th of November until Christmas Eve. A peal was rung on Christmas Eve and a muffled peal on New Years Eve. Hand-bell ringers from Horton-cum-Studley, the Gomm family came to entertain around the village on Christmas Eve with their hand-bells. I think they collected more drink than money. Sunday dinners were cooked in the bakery (in Church Street), immediately after morning service the men made their way to the bake-house to collect their dinners, the cost 1 (old) penny. Water was drawn from wells. Most cottages had an open range on which to do their cooking.

I started work at the age of 13 years for Mr Guy Thompson at Woodperry as a stable lad. the hours were from 6.30am to 5.00pm for six days a week and for 3 hours on Sundays. My wages to begin were 5 shillings (25 pence) per week. Most men worked on the farms, whilst the girls left home to enter domestic service. Most villagers kept a pig, and Church Street men kept theirs in a row of sties at the lower end of the street below the cottage where Mrs Venables lives .

(now sold and called Meadow Cottage,). When the pigs were killed the cottagers cured the meat in brine and afterwards took the hams and sides to hang in the bakehouse to dry.

All allotment holders grew corn which was stored in a barn known as "Poor Peoples Barn". It was adjoining the public house and is now converted into a house owned by Mr Drew Clifton (now sold and called 'The Old Barn'). In the autumn all the corn owners gathered at the barn, hired a machine and the corn was threshed, this was a combined effort and usually took about 2 days. 50% of the corn was wheat, which was sent to the mill to be ground into flour and then used at home for cooking. The rest of the corn, chiefly oats was ground for pig food. Between 40 and 50 acres of allotments were cultivated by the villagers. Allotments were situated at West End under Noke Wood, Spring Hill and Hall's Hill between Otmoor Lane and Beckley Park, Little Lintz and Big Lintz (sometimes spelt Lince) which today is the Recreation Ground, and Park Allotments by the side of Stowood. Today there are no allotments.

There were three village carriers, Mr Willis who went to Oxford on Mondays, Wednesdays, Fridays and Saturdays. Mr Lambourne and Mr Sumner on Wednesdays and Saturdays. They left Beckley at 9.00am and returned at 6.00pm. Fare 6d return (2½p). Since about 1927 buses have been coming to Beckley on Wednesdays, Fridays and Saturdays when the fare was 10d return (about 4p today). The return fare now (1960) is 4 shillings (20 p), (and now in 1998, £2.60 !)

The Post Office and shop combined was owned by Mr Harry Wing, who also did boot-making and repairs. Another food shop was in High Street and owned by Mrs Betsy

211

Coleman who bought pigs locally, had one killed each week and sold the joints to the villagers. Betsy Colemans brother killed all the pigs for the surrounding district and was known as Butcher Coleman. The blacksmiths shop owned by Mr Frank Auger is still standing in Otmoor Lane, although the forge has been taken away. The carpenter, wheelwright and undertaker was Mr Bailey Wakelin who lived in Cripps Cottage, he retired in 1918 and bought Upper Park Farm.

The nearest doctor was at either Islip or Wheatley and as there was no transport it meant quite a walk to the surgery.

Beckley Oddfellows Feast was held on the last Thursday in July. It commenced with the villagers meeting the Oakley Band on the Woodperry Road at 11.00am. From there all paraded to a service in the Church. At noon a dinner, cooked and served by the publican, was held in the barn opposite the Abingdon Arms. The dinner was followed by speeches and at

5.00pm the band assembled and paraded around the village when a collection was made.

Daily papers were first delivered in Beckley in 1911. A postal service was once a day. The postman Mr Giles, walked from Oxford, delivering mail to Elsfield and Stowood on the way to Beckley, and returned to Oxford with the collected mail in the evening. Later Mr Giles delivered the mail and returned to Oxford with the collected mail at 10.30am. In the afternoon another postman from Oxford did the same journey on a bicycle, delivering the mail at 2.30pm, collecting and returning to Oxford at 5.00pm.

Advice to my Grandson:-
Listen to, and follow the advice of your parents.

Harry L. Newell 1960.
Updated prices and subsequent changes of names and ownership of properties are added in brackets.

Harry's description of the Oddfellows Feast reminds me of a story concerning the band parade around the village. Ostensibly carried out to collect funds for the Society, the march included frequent stops at the cottages along the way for liquid refreshment, which eventually brought about a deterioration in the standards of marching and musical interpretation with increasingly hilarious results (apparently Beckley's home-made brews were highly potent !). It was said that on one occasion the band turned down Church Street but the bass drummer at the back, being some-what short in stature, a little deaf and no doubt peering through an alcoholic haze, turned the opposite way and continued on up New Inn Road still vigorously beating his drum and oblivious to the fact that he was on his own!

Ted Hall's pony and trap.

Transport Tales.

The days when horses were the main means of transport are recalled in the story of a horse and trap owned by Ted Hall, publican of the Abingdon Arms who farmed at Grove Farm until shortly before his death in 1966 at the age of 90 years. Ted travelled in the trap every Wednesday to Oxford Cattle Market. On his return he regularly called in to the

214

White Hart pub in Old Marston for refreshment. When Ted was unable to go and someone else took the trap to market, the pony, on the return journey would not pass the White Hart yard entrance, until he was allowed to enter the yard, and briefly stop, he refused to continue home to Beckley.

In this day and age, we tend to think that the traffic of earlier years was much quieter, but with the roads being a rougher finish, the carts having iron rimmed tyres, together with the clatter of the horses shoes, this was not necessarily the case. Steps were taken however to make life, or rather death quieter. When Mrs Lambourne, who lived in the house next to the Abingdon Arms, lay dying, straw was spread thickly across the road in front of the house to quieten the noise of passing traffic. This caring occurrence was quite usual in those circumstances and was carried out up to the time of the outbreak of the Second World War.

I recall Ted Hall's big 'Oxfordshire' farm waggons drawing the loads of harvest sheaves down to Grove Farm. Coming down into the village from New Inn Road the carter would struggle to hold back the horses, the wheels would have large iron skids placed under them to slow the waggon down, the skids and wheels emitted showers of sparks and by the time Church corner was reached were glowing bright red with heat. Great care had to be exercised in removing the skids before the waggons moved on up the lane into the farm and as the risk of fire was great in the wooden waggons and their loads, it was usual for buckets of water to be kept at the bottom of the lane to cool down the skids. The waggons were unloaded and the sheaves stacked in the rickyard behind the barn, until such times that threshing was carried out. The waggons were magnificent, sturdily built and beautifully painted, the body yellow and the inside and wheels red.

Growing up in Beckley   by Primrose Edwards

Beckley School, before breaking up for the Christmas holidays was always an exciting place to be. Miss Rosie Higgs who lived in Beckley and Miss Joan Beesley, who cycled from Oxford, ran the school together. At Christmas they made a great big cracker of red paper and filled it with presents. Arthur Payne helped by hanging the cracker from the ceiling, each child was given a present on the day we broke up.

Other happy times were spent in Beckley Methodist Chapel, by the pond (now a dwelling). A small team, Douglas Brazil, Arthur Cripps and their girl friends came from Headington and decided to start a Sunday School in the afternoon. Evening services were held at 7 o'clock. Men and Women Lay readers would attend, cycling out from places all around Oxford. I loved the Sankey hymns.

We had trips to the sea, and during the week 'Bun fights' as we called them. In Summer we played in my fathers field on Woodperry Road. We had dances in Beckley School, 'Tom Sumner's Band' would play, with Harry Whiting on the drums and Ron Clarke on the Bass. We had one character, Granny Eeles, who had a remarkable memory. When we had concerts she could recite poetry for half an hour or more.

Open air services were held outside the Abingdon Arms. Canon Swainson, the church vicar, often joined us and said how much he enjoyed them. Harvest Festival was another delightful time, the fruits and vegetables were auctioned off on the following day. Mr Boulter from Headington came out with his horse and cart, and bought all that was left over.

Primrose Edwards 1998 (Formerly Hall)

relatively short periods when the carrier was in the driving seat until the approach to Marston, the conversation was mainly between familiars, and in the local dialect much interspersed with "bi'st thee" and "bain't thee" as well as the ubiquitous "Aaarrh" of assent or confirmation.

By the time the bus service came to Beckley I was old enough to cycle , so the fact that the bus time table was more a matter of which days, rather than which hours did not concern me, It was though, these cycling days which helped fix in my mind the oft-told fact that the village was truly "on the road from nowhere in particular to somewhere else as doesn't matter". It is true that there are the nearby "Staarnn" and " 'orton come-cuddle- me " not forgetting Noke "where nobody spoke", not like Beckley where "um arnsers d'reckley".

Charles Payne

Cricket in 'The Grove' before World War Two

An outing to the seaside. 1960's

Chapter Seventeen

Changing Times

When one looks back through the parish baptism records at the occupations of the fathers of the infants, it is easy to follow the radical changes that have taken place in the patterns of employment, and therefore the population in our village, in the period of just over the last 100 years. In the 19th century the majority of the fathers trades recorded were farm labourers, with just a scattering of other country jobs such as groom, bailiff, blacksmith, wheelwright, coachman, game keeper and of course farmers and smallholders. Then there were the 'service' trades the baker, postman, publican, carrier, shoemaker, shopkeeper, carpenter and police officer - yes, we had our own village 'bobby' in days past, of which more later. In the period from 1882 until 1899 there were 160 baptisms of which 98 fathers were recorded as farm workers. Sadly the baptism records also show the high mortality rate amongst infants and children in the eighteenth and nineteenth centuries.

After the First World War and up to 1938/9, farm workers continued to dominate, reflecting the importance of agriculture in the village economy, but other trades such as mechanics, tool makers, trimmers, welders, and sheet metal workers were beginning to appear in the parish records showing that people were travelling to Cowley to the burgeoning car factories. The period during and after the Second World War saw the greatest changes in population and employment patterns in Beckley, As villagers returned from war service many former farm workers were not willing to go back to the land and were lured by the high wages offered in the Cowley factories. It was indeed fortunate that these years coincided to some extent with the mechanisation of agriculture which meant that fewer men were needed to tend the land. At the same time due to the increasing affluence of the nation, and the desire to live in more pleasant surroundings (and who could blame them?), together with the fact the population was becoming more mobile meant that a distance to travel to work was no longer a problem. Houses in the village were purchased by more people from the towns, many in professional occupations and some commuting daily quite long distances to their places of work. In consequence house prices rocketed and many of the offspring of old Beckley families could not afford to buy or rent houses in order to stay in the village, thus forcing them to seek cheaper accommodation elsewhere, which together with the fact there were no longer any jobs and few facilities in the village meant that most of the 19th century family names gradually disappeared.

In 1965 the Beckley Women's Institute booklet included an analysis of the jobs done by people in the parish. The figures included adults over 21 but not housewives, regular part-timers are included but not casual workers. The break down shows that 49 people worked in Beckley, 83 away from the village and 48 were retired. Of those working in Beckley :-

21 owned or managed farms or smallholdings.
13 were agricultural, forestry or estate workers.
 1 was a publican.

3 were builders.

1 was a baker.

1 was a glazier.

2 were school helpers.

7 were small traders.

Of those working elsewhere:-

17 worked for Pressed Steel.

9 worked for Morris Motors.

15 worked for small firms in the Oxford area.

6 worked for the University.

7 worked for other educational bodies.

4 worked for the County Council.

5 worked for the Oxford Hospitals.

4 were builders.

4 owned small businesses.

4 were sales representatives.

2 were servicemen.

2 were civil servants.

1 worked for the GPO.

1 was a solicitor.

Also listed were the farms as they were then:-

Farm	Owner	Farmer
Beckley Park	Mr Fielding	Mr Fielding.
Upper Park	Mr J.Wakelin	Mr J.Wakelin.
Church Corner	Mr C.H.Wakelin.	MrC.H.Wakelin.
Lower Farm	Miss Field	Mr Talbot.
Grove Farm	Mrs Cooke	"
Folly Farm	Brasenose	Mr Cox.
New Inn Farm	"	Mr Tompkins.
Lodge Farm	"	Mr Soanes.
Royal Oak Farm	"	"

225

In 1965 the total population was 382, of whom 94 were under twenty one. The oldest inhabitant was Mrs Cooke at 93 years of age.

How then do these figures compare with today ?

Thirty-five years on from the WI survey, we have a population comprising many more professional occupations than before, and with houses coming on to the market commanding ever higher prices. There have been no major housing developments in the parish other than a small one at

Manor Farm granary 1960

Beckley Court (older Beckley residents remembering when gravel was extracted there, still tend to call it 'The Pit'!). The population has been enlarged by the establishment of a residential caravan park of 54 dwellings at Wick Farm, on the edge of and accessed from Barton Estate Headington, but just inside Beckley and Stowood Parish. Their geographical situation means that Wick Farm residents probably identify and associate more with Headington than Beckley, it being truly 'Beckley's outpost of empire'. For the purpose of comparison with 1965, figures for the caravan park are not included.

In the national survey of 1991 the population of Beckley and Stowood parish was 584 which of course included Wick Farm. In making a direct comparison with the 1965 figures, there is inevitably a measure of approximation in the conclusions, but nevertheless the results show clearly how the village population has changed. 191 survey sheets were given out and returns received from 167 households giving a response rate of over 87% which apparently is a much higher figure than normally expected from this type of exercise. Results show that 101 residents were under 18 years of age and 88 were retired (nearly double those of 1965). It will be noticed that apart from the increase in population numbers, there are now far more people holding jobs, this is probably due to more partners holding full or part time occupations. The discrepancy in numbers between those surveyed and the following lists is accounted for by some residents having two or more occupations, and therefore those in this situation appear on both lists.

The oldest inhabitant at the time of writing is Mrs Creese who is 95 years old.

Of those working in Beckley :-

10 own, manage or work on farms.
 1 is a gamekeeper.
 1 is a stable manager.
 2 are partners in a Garden nursery.
 1 artist/illustrator.
 3 run a market garden.
 5 are school assistants.
 1 is a housekeeper/personal assistant.
 1 is a nanny. 1 is a carer.
11 own and run small businesses from home.
 2 are secretaries/clerical workers.
 5 are builders and/or property developers.
 1 is a music producer/comp-director.
 1 is a music teacher.
 1 repairs and restores china.
 2 are freelance film cameramen.
 1 is a freelance theatre director.
 1 is a freelance Journalist, writer and broadcaster.
 1 is an architectural surveyor.
 4 are authors. (in addition to their normal jobs)
 1 is a bar manager.
 1 is a chef.
 1 looks after the village hall.
And 20 chose to call themselves housewives.

It is significant that whereas in 1965 the people working in Beckley mainly worked in or around the village, in 1999 many of the ones above whilst having their business base at home often travel long distances (several overseas) in the course of their jobs. There is no longer a village baker, and the Royal Oak farm shop is the only retail food outlet. Beckwood Nurseries has been boosted by the take over by a local family. The Abingdon Arms has been refurbished, and has a good restaurant. The owner does not reside in the village but has a live-in manager.

Of those working elsewhere :-

16 are doctors, surgeons, consultants or GP's.
2 are dentists.
7 work in health care , therapists or hygienists.
1 artist/illustrator.
3 own, run or work in restaurants.
2 run farms away from the village.
12 are nurses or other NHS workers.
8 are consultants in management, property or computing.
21 are company directors or chief executives.
1 is a town planner.
1 music teacher.
1 is a piano tuner.
19 own or run businesses.
4 are in marketing.
2 are social workers.
2 are carpenters, 1 is a bricklayer, 1 is an engineer.
10 are teachers for the local authority or private schools.
1 is a Deputy Headmaster
1 is Principle of a College of FE.
6 are journalists, reporters, editors or copywriters.
4 are solicitors, 1 is a trainee solicitor.
1 is a legal secretary.
33 are academics - professors, tutors, and/or in research or administration.
2 work for colleges.
3 are accountants.
1 is a bank clerk.

1 is a secretary.
1 is a garden designer, 1 is a gardener.
2 work on overseas development.
2 work for the local authority.
1 is a Building Society manager.
3 are in Property management and development.
3 are surveyors.
1 is a sub-postmaster, 1 is a sub-postmistress, 1 is a postman.
1 is a trainee cameraman.
1 is a Councillor representing the area on County and District Councils.
21 are students (over the age of 18) at colleges of FE or University's.
2 work at the Cowley Rover car plant.
1 is a Justice of the Peace.
1 is a Police Surgeon.
1 is a Judge.
1 is a Police Officer in the Metropolitan Police at Heathrow Airport.

The shrinking size of the car factories is reflected by the numbers employed there, in 1965 Beckley had 26 working at Cowley, in 1999 just two!

The agricultural scene has also changed whereby few of the old farms are now occupied by a resident farmer and his family, many of the houses having been sold and now lived in by non farming families. Where houses have gone 'private' often the barns and other farm buildings have been converted into domestic dwellings. In such instances the farmland has been either sold off or contracted out to other farms so there has been very little if any, reduction in available agricultural land. The list is now as follows:-

Farm house	Owner	Land.
Beckley Park.	Lord and Lady Kneadpath.	Farmed by owners.
Middle Park.	House Privately owned.	Separate.
Upper Park.	House privately owned.	Separate.
Church Corner.	House privately owned.	Let by Wakelin Family.
Lower Farm.	House privately owned	Contracted.
Grove Farm	House privately owned.	Separate.
Folly Farm.	J.Cox Farms Ltd.	Cox Family.
New Inn Farm.	House privately owned.	Separate.
Lodge Farm.	House privately owned.	Separate.
Royal Oak Farm.	House privately owned new farmhouse and shop built.	Soanes family
Foxhill Farm.	John Cherry.	John Cherry.

Redways Farm   No house, this was originally a smallholding worked by Danny Goodgame who between the wars grew vegetables and kept pigs. It has now been developed into a large pig rearing enterprise by the Eadle family . Some farms employ workers from outside the parish which of course are not shown on the comparison.

So Beckley has evolved a pattern of change that has provided a very different range of occupations. The close proximity of the University and the Oxford Hospitals has had a great effect on the village population, replacing the farms and motor works as major employers. Many residents working in the medical and academic sector are important and distinguished people in their own particular fields.

To return to the village 'bobby' mentioned in the first paragraph, in 1907 the constables name was Arthur Baker, and in 1922 Fred Bond. The police 'station' being in the eastern half of what is now 'High Corner House' which was then two cottages. The last resident Police Constable who was in Beckley from 1923 until 1930 was Ernest Stevens. PC Stevens daughter Mary, who now lives at Adderbury, recalls an occasion when her father had to go to Oxford in his little Austin Seven car to take a man he had arrested to the main

Police Station, Mary's mother sat with them in the car holding a truncheon and with instructions to "give him one" if the suspect tried to escape.

Mary, daughter of the last Beckley Constable outside the village 'police station' 1925.

232

Beckley Reflects

So - Beckley has reflected on its past, is there then one thing about which it can be said - "that was the biggest reason for change"? - There are many factors that brought about a gradual departure from an economy based almost entirely on the soil with most of the houses and land owned by two prosperous landlords, to one where residents have freedom of choice, work here, there and everywhere mainly away from the village returning to homes they own themselves. All this started by changes in peoples attitudes and expectations, from the Commoners, their way of life badly affected by the Act of Enclosure, the uncertainty of continuity of work and tenure inherent in the 'tied' system, the revolution in farming methods by the introduction of mechanical power, through the horrors and privations experienced in two major World Wars and finally the period of financial prosperity brought about by better educational opportunities and full employment. All of these factors have contributed to the changes occurring in Beckley. Over a period of time changes are inevitable and Beckley cannot avoid them, but can those who succeed us expect as much radical change over the next one hundred or so years ? It will take a brave man (or woman) to speculate on what might happen, but meanwhile, never let us forget our past! ....

Beckley - Reflect On!

George and Elizabeth Hudson outside their cottage in Church Street

Acknowledgements.

Thank you to the following who have provided articles, information, photographs, other material and help, permission to publish, and most importantly advice, without all of which this book could not have been completed. They are listed alphabetically and not in any order of priority.

Airlife Publishing Ltd, publishers of 'One Wing High ' by Harry Lomas. John Amor, Kidlington (a former Head Teacher of Beckley School). Mary Barton, Adderbury. Beckley Parish Council. Beckley Parochial Church Council. Beckley Women's Institute. Beckley Youth Club. Eddie Birch, Curator, Oxford BT Museum. Bob Bixby, Beckley. Revd. Dr. William Brierley, (Team Vicar Beckley). Bill Broomfield, Beckley. Mike Bundock, Herne Bay, Kent. Peter and Janet Carter, Beckley. Violet Charlett, Headington (formerly of Beckley). Robert Cooke, Gillingham, Kent. John Cox, Beckley. Michael Davie, (Weidenfeld and Medson, The Orion Publishing Group). Rev. Anthony De-Vere, Headington (a former Vicar of Beckley). Primrose Edwards, Beckley. Niall Ferguson, Beckley. Len Ferris, Holborn, London. Peter and Anne Gibbons, Beckley. Albert and Mary Girdler, Beckley. Steve Holliday, RSPB. Simon Hogg, Beckley. Florrie Kettle, Cirencester. Lady Amanda Kneadpath, Beckley Park. Brenda Knight, Stanton St John. Viscount Knutsford, Exeter. Jack Lankester, Beckley. Neil Lambert, RSPB, Otmoor Reserve. Judith Lea, Beaconsfield. Mary and Roy Longthorne. Lincoln, (formerly of Beckley). Ruth Mandeno (nee, Dawber), New Zealand, (formerly of Beckley). Jane Markham, Beckley. Nicholas Mynheer, Horton-cum-Studley. Col Lucas, TAVRA. The late Harry Newell, Beckley (by courtesy of his grandson Michael Woodward). William North, Oddington. Ordnance Survey (Crown Copyright). The Centre for Oxfordshire Studies and The Photographic Archive, The Library Service, and Oxfordshire Archives (all departments of Oxfordshire County Council). Oxford and County Newspapers. The Oxford Times. Mrs E.K. Parnell, Oxford. Roger and Charles Payne, Belper, Derbyshire. Phillimore and Co Ltd, Publishers, Chichester, Sussex. Frank Ratford, Beckley. Vanessa Ross, Beckley. Public Record Office Kew. Bill Quartermain, Beckley. The late Arthur Rawlinson, Beckley. Scholastic Souvenir Co, Blackpool. Mark Seaman, Imperial War Museum. The late Col Ted Shephard, TAVRA. Horton-cum-Studley. Tony and Sara Strong,

Beckley. Malcolm Sumner, Beckley. David Talbot, Beckley. Baron Tweedsmuir, Hornton, Banbury. Dr Stanley R.J.Woodell, Oakley, Bucks. Heather Whetter, English Nature. Gilly Weaver, Noke, (formerly of Beckley). Brian and Gill Westbury, Beckley. Jan Weller, Beckley. Barbara Wharton, Beckley. Elizabeth Wheeler, Beckley. The late Hector Wheeler, Beckley. Phyllis Wheeler, Beckley. Eileen and Len Williams, Beckley. David Wing, Headington, (formerly of Beckley). John and Ann Wing, Beckley. Finally all the people of Beckley who kindly took part in the population survey.

Photographs.

Because of the absence of information on the originators of some of the photographs reproduced and despite efforts being made to trace them, I have been unable in these cases, to seek consent and I apologise for not being able to give due credit. I hope however, that in the event of anyone recognising their photographs, they would understand that I have tried to find them and in the circumstances would kindly consider granting retrospective permission.

The names of those kindly giving permission to reproduce photographs, drawings and maps together with the page numbers on which the images appear are as follows :

Mary Barton, 178 (by Scholastic Souvenir Co). 232. Beckley Parochial Church Council. 63.68. Beckley Women's Institute, 172. Beckley School, 173. Bob Bixby, 82.124 (Bottom). 137.143. Bill Broomfield, 25.48.49.51.106.113. Peter and Anne Gibbons, 223. Albert and Mary Girdler, 32.102.186 (by The Oxford Times). 204. 207. Simon Hogg 79. Vera Kastner, 21. Florrie Kettle, 84. 85. 86. Judith Lea, 94. The Late Margaret Lightbody, 61. Mary and Roy Longthorne, 66. 91. Ruth Mandeno nee, Dawber, 64. Nicholas Mynheer, 74.75.76. William North, 9. 41. Ordnance Survey (Crown Copyright), 11. Oxfordshire County Council, Oxfordshire Archives. 44. Oxford and County Newspapers, 138. Mrs E.K.Parnell, 97. Roger Payne 1.92.203.209. The Late Arthur Rawlinson 125. 127. RSPB, 47. Scholastic Souvenir Co, Blackpool, Malcolm Sumner, 131.134.135.161.221.222. Dr Stanley R.J.Woodell, 50. Gilly Weaver, 83.115.169 (Chapter heading).. Brian and Gill Westbury, 140.141.159.165.168. JanWeller, 187. 206. The Wheeler family,

Frontcover,3.7.8.17.18.20..23.26.28.40(Bottom).71.103.104.144 (Top).145.146.147.153.156.174. 198.199.205.208.214.234. Eileen and Len Williams, 5. 180 (by Scholastic Souvenir Co). David Wing, 226 (enhanced by Bill Broomfield). John and Ann Wing, 6.13.29.35.40 (Top). 46. 124 (Top). 132. 144 (Bottom). 158.169.177.188.191.193.212.

Many of the photographs shown are from postcards sent or received by the Hall/Senior family early in the 20th century. They have stamps from and are postmarked in the reign of Edward VII (1901 - 1910).

I wish to put on record my special thanks to Bill Broomfield (my honorary publisher) for his artistic flair, photographic skills and electronic wizardry as well as invaluable advice and counsel.

It should also be mentioned that the whole of the work on this book (apart from printing and binding costs) has been on a voluntary basis and that all professional publishing and other fees have been waived for the benefit of the Parish.

PMW. 1999.

About the Editor

Peter Wheeler has lived in Beckley all his life. He grew up in the house his father built in Church Street and now lives in the cottage next door with his wife Phyllis who is also a lifelong resident (they were childhood sweethearts). He served in the Royal Navy during World War II mainly in the Far East and retired in 1987 after over 40 years as an engineer with the Southern Electricity Board.